DO-IT-YOURSELFER'S GUIDE TO CHAINSAW USE & REPAIR

No. 892
$8.95

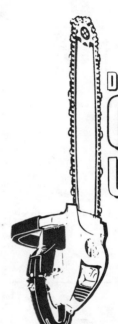

DO-IT-YOURSELFER'S GUIDE TO
CHAINSAW
USE & REPAIR

BY CHARLES SELF

TAB BOOKS
Blue Ridge Summit, Pa. 17214

FIRST EDITION

FIRST PRINTING— MARCH 1977

Copyright © 1977 by TAB BOOKS

Printed in the United States
of America

Library of Congress Cataloging in Publication Data

Self, Charles R
   Do-it yourselfer's guide to chainsaw use & repair.

   Includes index.
   1. Chain saws. I. Title.
TS851.S3   621.9'3   77-1731
ISBN 0-8306-7892-1
ISBN 0-8306-6892-6 pbk.

Preface

Chain saws for the homeowner have become as common as screwdrivers and twice as useful. Prices have dropped because people recognize that the chain saw is an exceptionally useful tool.

With a chain saw you can build lawn furniture or cut firewood or build fences. You can clear land, cut firebreaks, trim trees or sculpt wood. With a few accessories you can even mill your own lumber, dirt cheap. You can do a thousand useful jobs that other saws can't even touch.

This book is for those who want to get the best use out of their chain saws. It tells you how to use your saw—safely and effectively. It shows you how to keep it running smoothly for its full life. Repair and maintenance chapters will enable you to handle any problem, from carburetor adjustment to major overhaul.

All systems are discussed in depth. There are chapters on overhauls, carburetion, ignition, chain care, troubleshooting, and accessories. And there's plenty of information on how to use your chain saw—how to saw lumber, how to fell trees, how to cut firewood, how to use your chain saw for useful, imaginative projects.

Charles Self

Contents

Chapter 1

Selecting A Chain Saw

Selecting A Chain Saw

Chain saw selection used to be simple. You bought the saw you could afford and used it. There weren't very many brands and probably just one or two models per brand. All were designed primarily for professional use with little thought given to the occasional user. They were bulky, heavy, hard to start and use, and often required wheels to move them from one tree to another. The original chain saws were suitable for not much more than heavy-duty lumbering.

The problem now is entirely different. Small homeowner chain saws have been in existence for not much more than a decade. Engine, or powerhead, weight has dropped to under 6 pounds in a few cases. Since many of the early saws weighed several hundred pounds, the advances are obvious, as are the advantages.

In 1948, the first 50-pound chain saw was introduced. The next year, the weight had dropped to 25 pounds, and an all-position carburetor was added. By 1962, chain saws had not dropped very much more in weight, but sales of the lightest professional models were starting to be made to homeowners. Then in 1965, the first 10-pound chain saw was developed. By 1968, the 6-pound chain saw was with us, and by 1970 a 6 pounder for the "occasional user" market was in existence.

Today's heavy duty saws seldom weigh more than 25 pounds, while some of the little 8-inch electric models are well under 6 pounds. Of course, they are suitable only for rather light work such as pruning trees and cutting down saplings.

Today there are more than a dozen companies making chain saws for the occasional user on a worldwide basis. Two companies, Homelite and McCulloch, dominate the market in this country (and several others), but other large companies such as Pioneer (Outboard Marine Corporation), Beaird-Poulan (Emerson Electric), and Remington (DESA Industries) are fighting hard for chunks of the huge market. Other brands include Jonsenreds, Oleo Matic, Sears, Skil, Solo, Stihl, Partner, Wen, and Echo.

It's possible to find a given chain saw size manufactured in as many as six different forms by a single maker! The popular mid-range saw with a 16-inch guide bar is a good example; Homelite offers at least seven such saws and McCulloch eight (of course, almost all can be purchased with other size guide bars, too). Poulan has saws with 17-inch guide bars.

Mini saws, those little powerhouses which seem to be found in nearly every garage or workshop in the country , are being built by most large companies. Here, two or more saws with 12- or 10-inch guide bars can be found usually with a 14-inch guide bar included in the catalog. Not many of the major chain saw manufacturers, however, are now carrying a line of electric *and* gas powered chain saws (Skil, Sears and Remington are the major exceptions), but there are still a good number of these saws to choose from in the 10- and 12-inch range (Figs. 1-1 and 1-2). I wouldn't recommend the 8-inch models to anyone though, since they are super light-duty

Fig. 1-1. A Skil Model 1602 14-inch electric chain saw.

Fig. 1-2. A Homelite XL-2 chain saw.

saws which retain disadvantages of the bigger saws (except weight) but few of the advantages.

Chain saw selection has now become a matter of deciding on a saw size which will do the job you need done, then finding one from a manufacturer that produces a saw that fits your hands and needs as perfectly as possible.

Consideration of your needs is paramount in proper chain saw selection. Buying less saw than you need will save a few dollars at the outset but will cause major problems later. The saw will just not do a good job on the work you need to complete. It will waste time, energy, and money. Buying a larger saw than you need is as big a problem as buying too small a saw, for almost the same reasons. Though the oversized and overpowered saw may easily handle all the cuts you will ever make, it will use more fuel, whether gas or electricity, and it will cost a lot more at the outset. Replacement chains will cost more. Replacement guide bars will cost more. Sharpening will cost more and take longer. Any internal parts are likely to be larger and more expensive. And an oversized saw is tougher to lug around in the woods. For example, one of my saws has two roller nose guide bars, a 16-inch bar (standard with that model), and a 24-inch oversize bar for the occasional oversize tree. The 24-inch bar, though, is right at the power limit for this particular saw, which means that the saw will bog down too quickly and too easily in dense, seasoned wood. Also, the longer guide bar makes the saw harder to handle. I'm more likely to bump into something with the longer bar nose, causing kickback. The saw is also harder to handle when walking through, or working in, thick brush.

14

The oversize bar and chain is considerably heavier as well, so the balance of the saw is severely changed, and not for the better (this may not be a factor with saws especially designed to use a longer guide bar, however).

Smaller saws are available, of course, and in many cases are recommended, but to me the best all-around guide bar size is 16 inches (Fig. 1-3 and 1-4). Different brands jump this an inch or so in one direction or the other; there are 15-inch bars, 17-inch bars, even a few 18-inch units floating around. Practical guide-bar lengths for homeowners include 12 inch, 14 inch, 16 inch, 20 inch, and 24 inch. Anything smaller or larger is generally impractical in terms of either utility or cost. Those very tiny saws lack the depth of cut needed to take down trees greater than 18 inches in diameter, while the larger saws are heavier, much harder to handle, and a great deal more costly.

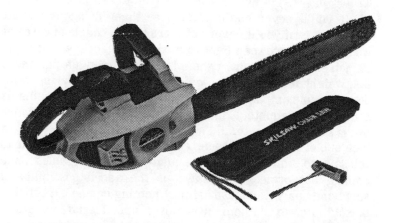

Fig. 1-3. A Skil Model 1616 16-inch gasoline chain saw with sheath and combination tool.

As an example of expense, assume a Super EZ costs around $225 with the standard 16-inch guide bar. If you move up only as far as Homelite's 350 Auto, about the bottom of their professional line with a 16-inch guide bar, it will cost you another $85. With a 24-inch guide bar, that cost will rise another $30 (Fig. 1-5). Going down the scale to an XL-2 with a 12-inch guide bar will drop costs to little more than half the price of the EZ (if the XL-2 is on sale!). These prices are not meant to be accurate indications of what you'll have to pay at this time, but are used to show a range of prices one might pay

Fig. 1-4. A Homelite XL12 16-inch gasoline chain saw.

for different saw types. Your best bet is to consider the price differentials as a percentage. The smallest saw costs about half what the mid-range saw costs, while the next model up the line can cost half again as much as the mid-range saw. That's a range of 100%, or nearly $200.

If you'll never cut a tree more than 18 inches in butt thickness, or if you'll never cut more than a couple of cords of wood, or do more than light to moderate chain saw work, the 12-inch size is excellent. I should probably mention that these lightweight chain saws do not present the buyer with ultra-cheap components. Bearing support in the engine is completely adequate. Engine life with even heavy homeowner use is very long, up to and sometimes well past ten years. In fact, one of the many reasons chain saw manufacturers like to sell saws to professional lumbermen—a lot of companies make nothing but professional saws—is the added possibility of supplying spare parts. But almost nothing can be expected to be sold later to the homeowner user since after ten years of use, most people have to discard the old saw and buy a new one. The only extras companies usually sell are guide bars,

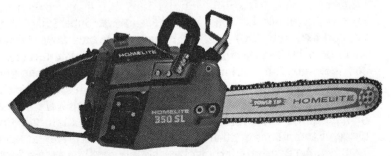

Fig. 1-5. Homelite's 350 SL chain saw.

chains, an occasional sharpening tool, oil used in premixing the fuel, or, perhaps, chain oil.

Look around you. If you plan to prune only half a dozen trees a year, cut just a little firewood, or do relatively light jobs with your saw, select a 12-inch model from the manufacturer you prefer. Twelve-inch saws will cost from $10 to $40 more than a 10-inch model, but will provide, usually, a fair degree of added power in addition to that extra 4 inches of cut (any chain saw will cut approximately double its advertised bar length. If you expect to cut large branches, prepare more than a couple cords of wood each year, or generally do heavy work with the tool, the 16-inch guide bar chain saw is for you. If you expect to do land clearing or other heavy-duty wood cutting, look at the bottom end of the professional lines. These chain saws are most often advertised for farm use. For fairly constant heavy duty, such saws will do a better job than the standard homeowner's 16-inch chain saw, even though they may have the same size guide bar. Too, the heavier-duty saws will be designed with extra power, and they will be balanced to use a bar up to 24-inches in length, possibly even more.

Such heavy-duty saws have more power, heavier components, and better vibration control. McCulloch's Power Mac 6 Automatic has a 2 cubic inch displacement engine, while a Mac 10-10 Automatic 16-inch saw, the present bottom of the McCulloch professional line, offers for about $30 to $35 more a 3.3 cubic inch engine plus a longer guide bar and chain. It would be possible to use a 20-inch guide bar on the Mac 10-10, but a 16-inch bar would be the maximum on the Power Mac 6 (a 14 inch bar is standard).

The top of McCulloch's professional line shows a much greater size and price differential, with a 7.5 cubic inch engine. Even with a short 14-inch guide bar and chain, the Super Pro 125C costs nearly $300 more than does the Power Mac 6! The Super Pro 125C is the most expensive saw McCulloch makes. Consider carefully before investing up to $500 in any chain saw. The same considerations apply to Homelite's line which ranges from the XL-2 with its 12-inch guide bar and very small engine to the 650 professional chain saw (Fig. 1-6) with a 16-inch bar and chain powered by a 6.1 cubic inch engine (the XL-2 has a 1.6 cubic inch displacement engine). A better buy for the homeowner, even the homeowner doing considerable

Fig. 1-6. Homelite's 650 professional chain saw with a 6.1 cubic inch engine.

wood cutting, would be a saw such as Homelite's 2.5 cubic inch Super EZ; it's about $100 more than the XL-2 but several hundred dollars less than the 650 professional.

It pays to also remember that professional chain saws, especially those with extra long guide bars, are going to weigh you down a lot more than even the largest homeowner's saw. With more weight to handle, you'll tire sooner.

Professional chain saws will usually zip through a log quickly. Much of that big engine and engine casing is devoted to withstanding the rigors of life under extreme conditions, those which consist of running eight to ten hours a day under heavy loads. Though one or two out of a score of homeowner's chain saws may see this sort of use once or twice a year, almost none will see such extreme wear and tear day in and day out for several years. Thus, homeowners simply do not need all that extra quality, weight, size, and cost. In fact, several professional woodcutters in my area, people who use a chain saw with almost the same intensity as do lumbermen in the North woods, use the lightweight saws. One friend is now using a Sears saw after finally wearing out his Homelite. Because Wayne gets anywhere from three to four years from these saws, he won't even consider spending over $250 for them. The heavy pro models are out as far as he's concerned. Another year to two of use just isn't worth the big price or the extra weight to sling around every day or the greater fuel consumption. Fortunately for Wayne, however, the wood around here, though almost all hardwood of some kind or another, is under 30 inches in trunk diameter. So there's no need for a chain saw with the power to drive a larger guide bar and chain combination, a factor often essential in selecting saws for major lumbering operations in other areas.

In other words, then, get the smallest chain saw that will do the job you want done with just a little power held in reserve. The result will be a savings in both money and energy for you.

Chain saws come with two types of power plants. All the gas engine chain saws use two-stroke engines that require you to mix gas and engine oil together before you put it in the gas tank. Electric chain saws, obviously, have electric motors. One maker, Skil, offers electric saws that will operate from either AC or DC sources.

Gas chain saws offer greater portability since there is no need to lug along hundreds of feet of extension cord or an alternator/generator unit. Gas saws also offer the buyer greater flexibility in guide bar size and engine power. Most electric chain saws are set up with 14-inch or shorter guide bars and are rated at under 2 horsepower.

Gasoline chain saws are no longer rated in horsepower. Manufacturers seem to have gotten together and decided they weren't going to get caught up in a Detroit-type contest reminiscent of the late '50s horsepower race. Don't automatically think that a saw with an engine twice as large is necessarily twice as powerful, for there is a point of diminishing return where the size of engine components begins to limit power output per cubic inch (such things as internal friction on larger bearing surfaces can waste power). Usually, though, it is safe to assume that a 3 cubic inch engine is nearly twice as powerful as a 1.5 cubic incher. Some manufacturers get more power out of small engines than others, but the difference is often relatively minor. Almost any well made, well designed gasoline-driven chain saw will produce sufficient power to drive its bar through the hardest wood at a reasonable pace—assuming the chain und guide bar are in good condition.

Electric chain saws present a few problems gasoline-driven saws do not, but they also offer advantages. First among the disadvantages is a limited operating range. If you wish to use your saw more than about 10 feet from a wall outlet, it is necessary to use an extension cord. That extension cord must be a heavy-duty model, not those skinny little types used for table lamps. Not a single one of the electric chain saws now on the market draws less than 12 amperes of current, which, when considering starting surge, is right up there at or near the limits of most 15-ampere circuits in a home. Therefore, to carry the current, the size of the extension cord must relate to its length, or the resistance along the wire will cause a severe voltage drop. For a 15-ampere rating, which should suit all electric chain saws now available, use a number 12 copper wire extension for runs up to 50 feet. From 50 to 100 feet, you'll need an extension cord with wire no smaller than number 10. If you move out from 100 to 150 feet, your wire number will rise to a number 8. From 150 to 250 feet away from the socket, you'll need number 6 extension wire. Beyond 250 feet, you'll need a truck to haul the number 4 wire you'll need! Number 4 wire is huge and very, very expensive. In fact, all extension cords larger in diameter than number 10 copper will almost certainly have to be made up specially and will cost a bit more than a small fortune. Sometimes the wire can cost more than the chain saw, particularly since electric chain saws tend to be priced 30 to 50 percent under comparable gasoline chain saws. Thus the practical limit for electric chain saw use would be about 100 feet from the power source if you wish to retain full motor power and cut down on the chances of overheating the motor. You might push that to an occasional 150 or even 200 feet with 10 gauge wire, but it isn't advisable.

The quietness of the electric chain saw is one of its prime advantages. If you've spent a day working in the woods with a gasoline-driven saw, you know how disturbing the noise can be. The electric saw is a great deal quieter.

The lack of noise helps to balance out another disadvantage of the electric chain saw: sooner or later you'll cut through the saw's power cord. Everyone I've ever known who has used an electric chain saw extensively for any period of time has done so.

Electric chain saws do not produce toxic fumes since there is no internal combustion engine kicking out carbon monoxide and other byproducts of incomplete combustion. Thus, an electric chain saw can safely be used indoors. The chain oil, if you push the saw too hard in the cuts, may smell up a room, but a gasoline-driven chain saw is flat out dangerous indoors unless *all* doors and windows are opened and a large fan is used to exhaust the fumes. Even then the gas saw is very unpleasant. If you do any chain sawing indoors—which on a nasty day can be a handy place to buck smaller logs for the fireplace—the electric chain saw is the saw to use. I wouldn't even start a gasoline driven saw indoors unless the house had no roof!

All chain saws are subject to damage from overheating. Electric chain saws are more prone to such damage; the windings on the electric motor are quite fine and can break down under extreme heat conditions. When an electric motor stalls, it still draws heat-producing current. A gasoline engine, on the other hand, lies dormant. In other words, if the chain saw is going to be subjected to more than periodic overloads, the best bet is a gasoline-driven saw.

No electric chain saw offers automatic oiling, which usually means the chain wears out, or dulls, quickly since it never gets quite enough oil. No one ever seems to remember to push the manual oiler button as often as it should be pushed, and those few who try end up with a very tired thumb.

Electric chain saws start instantly and need less regular maintenance than gasoline chain saws. Flick a switch and you go, with never a worry about carburetor adjustments or hard starting in cold weather. And electric chain saws are generally a pound or so lighter than similar size gasoline chain saws.

In some cases, it may pay to have both types, a feat made possible by the lower prices of electric chain saws, which now range from about $50 to $100. They're expected to stay close to that price range for some time to come. Even less expensive electric saws are available with 8 inch guide bars, but these have few uses beyond pruning small branches or cutting saplings.

When shopping around for a chain saw, consider the job to be done as well as the cost of the saw. In many cases, the gasoline powered chain saw will prove to be cheaper because no extras such as extension cords are needed. In other cases, gas-driven saw may be too dangerous to use (if its major use is to be indoors, an electric chain saw is the only choice you can make).

Check for the features you want, select the saw closest to the correct size in your price range and you should have few problems. If you have a certain size in mind, and the manufacturer you favor doesn't produce a saw of that size, go up one size. Slightly too much power and size is a bit better than slightly too little power and size.

On any gasoline-driven chain saw, an automatic oiler is a must. If you can always remember to flick the manual oiler button, there are a few models around that could possibly save you $10 or $20 by not including the automatic oiler. But auto oiling is generally to be preferred over manual oiling alone, as it usually results in the chain staying sharper longer, longer chain life, and increased guide bar life. The chain saw that provides both manual and automatic oiling is a good idea. Metered amounts of oil are delivered by the automatic oiler, but when you start slicing into some seasoned oak or hickory, the possibility of adding a fair amount of extra oil to the chain and bar becomes very important. It helps to reduce wear on the chain and lessen the amount of pressure you must bring to bear on the saw as it cuts into the wood.

If horsepower figures fascinate you, the average two-stroke chain saw engine can usually be listed as developing about 1 horsepower per cubic inch. Some may develop as much as 1.35 or a bit more for each cube, but the average is probably around one or just a bit more. By automotive standards, this may sound like spectacular power from a tiny engine, but by the standards of the small engine field, these power plants are decidedly understressed and designed to produce good torque characteristics rather than extreme horsepower figures. A great many small two-stroke engines in other applications (motorcycle racing, for instance) produce well over 2 horsepower per cubic inch—some nearly 3 horsepower per cube. Yamaha's 350cc road racer (about 21 cubic inch engine displacement) is claimed to produce nearly 54 horsepower; some top engine tuners get even more!

Look for an all-position carburetor. As far as I can discover, all chain saws made today have an all-position carb. Such a carburetor is essential to continued use as the chain saw is turned on its side, upside down, and all around. The chances of fuel starvation are good without an all-position carburetor.

Almost all modern chain saws will do a decent job, but for constant and heavy use the saw must have controls spaced so your hands fall naturally on them. The saw must also be balanced so it is easy to use, thereby cutting down on muscle strain and fatigue. Just about the only sensible way to find out which saw fits you best is to try as many different brands and models as you can. Don't forget, if one model in a particular brand doesn't fit your physique or handling style, the next model up or down the line just might do the job perfectly. If one brand doesn't have a chain saw with handling to suit you, move on to another and give that a try. There are certainly enough brands around to provide a wide selection.

Vibration level differences among models and brands can be extreme, too. The only check for vibration level is a use test, which is sometimes a bit difficult to arrange. Some dealers have demonstrators, others don't. Occasionally, you may have a friend who has a chain saw different from any others you've tried. Talk him into a test, if you can. The use test will also give you an indication of the noise level you'll have to contend with when the saw is in constant use. If no other way to get a use test exists, you can always search among tool rental companies until you locate one with the type of saw you want to check out.

So here are some things to look for in a chain saw: automatic oiling with backup manual oiling, an all-position carburetor, low noise, low vibration, comfortable controls, ease of handling. All of this should be added to and weighed against cost, size, and power.

Ease of handling will be strongly affected by the overall weight and balance of a chain saw. The lighter the chain saw, the greater the ease of handling, even with relatively poor saw balance. But the heavier the saw, the more important becomes the balance while in use. Test the saw by making cuts down from the top, up from the bottom, on its sides, and close to the ground.

How close to the ground you can cut can be important, so this check is necessary. With the saw turned on its side, see how close the guide bar will come to the ground. A guide bar that can be moved close to the ground aids general tight-spot maneuverability. It allows you to work closer to obstructions near the tree. A low cut, too, can often add a good-sized log butt to your firewood collection after the tree has been felled. Also, trimming brush around trees is easier.

Many chain saws come with the guide bar and chain in one package and the powerhead in another. Make sure you're getting the listed bar and chain for the powerhead and drive sprocket you are buying.

Select a roller nose bar, also known as a sprocket nose bar, if possible. This type of guide bar cuts down on chain friction as the chain travels over the most difficult parts of its journey. By cutting down on friction, the roller nose guide bar adds to both bar and chain life, cuts down slightly on engine power needs, and helps maintain cutting speed in heavy going. In addition, though the roller or sprocket nose guide bars cost a little more at the outset, they can be removed by drilling out a few rivets. Then a replacement nose can be slid into place and secured with new rivets set with a hammer. A new roller nose for your guide bar is a lot cheaper than a full bar of any type, whether hard nose or roller nose.

LIST OF CHAIN SAW TERMS

A chain saw consists of two separate units, the powerhead and the cutting unit (Fig. 1-7).

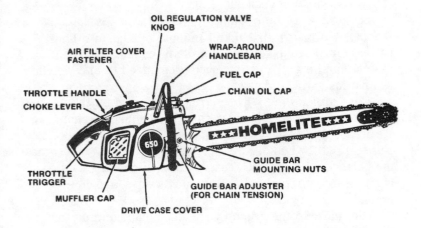

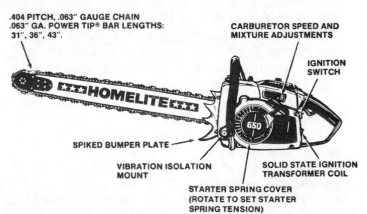

Fig. 1-7. Chain saw nomenclature. (Courtesy Homelite.)

Powerhead. The powerhead will contain either an air-cooled two-stroke engine or a universal electric motor. The drive shaft connects to a centrifugal clutch on homeowner chain saws, while some units made for professionals use a gear reduction drive instead of just the centrifugal clutch.

Cutting Unit. The cutting unit has a grooved guide bar on which the chain is carried. The chain is driven along the guide bar by a drive sprocket. It is the cutting teeth on the chain which do the actual work of cutting wood.

Guide Bar. Guide bars provide the track on which the chain runs, and, as such, are very important to proper saw operation. They must be in good condition and the proper size, called bar gauge width, to match the thickness of the chain's center link tangs. If the bar groove is too narrow, the chain will bind. If the groove is too wide, the chain will lean. The guide bar also has adjustment slots at the powerhead end and an oil hole that feeds oil to the chain.

Chain. A chain saw chain looks something like a bicycle or motorcycle chain (metal side plates riveted to rollers to form a continuous loop). Also riveted onto the side plates are the center drive tangs and the right and left teeth, or cutters. These teeth are the only parts of the saw which actually cut wood. Each chain is characterized in two ways: pitch and gauge. Sprocket pitch and chain pitch must match, for the pitch refers to the distance, in an arc, between the tips of the sprocket teeth. Too small a pitch means too much slip and wear. With too large a sprocket pitch, the drive tangs will not properly fit between the sprocket tangs and will cause excessive slip and wear. Chain gauge refers to the thickness of the center link tang.

Sprocket. A drive sprocket pulls the chain around the guide bar. A roller or sprocket nose on the guide bar must be the same size; it must have the same number of teeth and the same pitch as the drive sprocket. The sprocket nose simply provides a lowering of friction as it turns, which aids the chain in its trip around the guide bar.

Chapter 2
Engine Fundamentals

Engine Fundamentals

The power source for the modern chain saw will differ little from those used to run many other tools and accessories. Power is provided by either an internal combustion reciprocating engine running on a mixture of gasoline and oil or by a universal electric motor drawing 12 to 14 amperes (1320 to 1540 watts or about the same power requirement as a large toaster or waffle iron).

TWO-AND FOUR-CYCLE ENGINES

In the gasoline engine, the power is drawn from heat created by burning a mixture of gasoline, oil, and air. The fuel mixture is ignited by a spark plug. The burning takes place in a closed cylinder which contains a piston. Expansion resulting from the heat of combustion provides the pressure to force the piston downward. That piston is connected to a crankshaft by means of a connecting rod. The crankshaft turns as the piston is forced downward.

OPERATION

Two types of gasoline engines are in wide use today. The cycling of the engine types is quite different. In the more common four-stroke engine, each phase of operation; intake, combustion, power, and exhaust, requires one-half turn of the crankshaft, while the two-cycle, or two-stroke, engine goes through all four phases of operation in only a single turn of the crankshaft. Two-stroke engines predominate in the chain saw field, with only one or two manufacturers seriously considering using rotary, or Wankel, engines (Dolmar, in their line of professional chain saws, has recently introduced such a saw, but the price is well up into the $500 range, and only a few saws have been produced at this time). We can safely bypass the rotary engine and the standard four-stroke engine (except for a quick look at the basic Otto cycle).

In every internal combustion reciprocating engine, the following five things must happen for the engine to run.

1. **Intake**—A mixture of fuel and air is drawn or forced into the cylinder.
2. **Compression**—The fuel/air mixture is compressed as the piston rises in the cylinder.
3. **Ignition**—The fuel/air mixture is ignited by a timed electric spark (except diesels).
4. **Power**—The burning fuel/air mixture expands, moving the piston downward, turning the crankshaft.
5. **Exhaust**—The burned gases are exhausted from the cylinder as a prelude to a new intake of fuel/air mixture.

In a two-stroke engine, the five events take place during only a single turn of the crankshaft; that is, during only two strokes—one up and one down—of the piston. Every time the piston reaches the top of its stroke, the fuel/air mixture is fired, producing a power stroke.

Two-stroke engine theory, oddly enough for a device constructed so simply and with so few parts in comparison to four-stroke engines, is somewhat harder to understand than four-stroke engine theory. Part of the problem probably comes from the combining of several actions on each stroke, but the engine itself is a great deal simpler to work on.

Each function of the engine has not been labeled as clearly as it has in the four-stroke design. As an example, the crankcase in a four-stroke engine serves as a holding bin and source of lubricant for engine internal parts. In a two-stroke engine, the crankcase serves not as a holding place for lubricant, but as an air pump to force the fresh fuel/air mixture into the cylinder and as a storage and precompression area for that fuel/air mixture. The piston acts not only as a sealant for the combustion chamber, a pressurizer for gases in the crankcase, and as a valve for the exhaust ports, but also as a valve for the transfer ports and, in many engines, as a valve for the intake ports. All of this is piled on top of the piston's usual jobs.

Because there are no four-cycle valves to open and close the exhaust and intake ports, there is no valve train to add weight and require lubrication. The following discussion of the complete process in a reed-valve, crankcase-scavenged system will help you understand the operation better.

As the piston moves upward, the volume of the sealed crankcase grows larger. The crankcase pressure drops, drawing air into the carburetor. The carburetor mixes fuel with the incoming air, and this fuel/air mixture is then drawn through the reed valve into the crankcase. As all of this happens, the previous charge of fuel is compressed between the crown of the piston and the cylinder head. When the piston nears the top dead center of its travel, a timed spark ignites the fuel/air mixture.

Expansion of the burning fuel/air mixture forces the piston downward. This is called the power stroke. The reed valve closes, and the downward movement of the piston precompresses the fuel charge in the crankcase. As the piston crown nears a carefully calculated spot on the cylinder wall, the exhaust port in that cylinder wall is uncovered, thus allowing the burned products of combustion to escape. Further downward movement of the piston uncovers a transfer port which leads from the crankcase to the cylinder, allowing the precompressed fuel/air mixture to force most of the remaining products of combustion into the exhaust and fill the cylinder with a fresh fuel/air mixture. The piston then begins its upward travel, first sealing off the transfer port, then the exhaust port, and then recompressing the fuel/air mixture in readiness for the next ignition/power cycle.

The exhaust port leads the transfer port as the piston is on its downward stroke, but it follows the transfer port on the compression, or upward, stroke. It is for this reason that two-stroke engines are never as economical as four-stroke engines. Even with strictly controlled port timing, some waste of the incoming fuel/air charge must occur as it is forced out the exhaust port on the compression stroke of the piston. This also tends to add to air pollution, which is one reason Saab quit producing its three cylinder, two-stroke automobile several years ago. No one has yet managed to prevent this overlap and the resultant pumping of unburned fuel into the atmosphere.

The rotary valve can replace the reed valve in any two-stroke engine application, but the basic theory remains the same as long as the engine is the crankcase-scavenging type (pressurized crankcase gases force the rest of the burned mixture out of the cylinder as the piston rises).

Because the crankcase of a two-stroke engine is open to the atmosphere for a severely limited time (only when the fresh fuel/air charge is being drawn through the reed valve), any leakage in the crankcase seals becomes a major problem. It can cause anything from a severe loss of power to a total shutdown of engine operation, depending on the severity of the leak. A low crankcase compression reduces the chance of major and frequent problems with crankcase sealing. Because of inherent losses in porting, the crankcase compression will seldom exceed 1.3 to 1, so the actual pressure is quite mild, at least in relation to upper end engine compression ratios of 7 or 8 to 1.

Lubrication in two-stroke engines is as crictical as that in four-stroke engines. Most of the areas needing lubrication are located near the intake porting so the oil mixed with the gasoline sprays over these areas in a fine mist. This, by the way, is one of the major limiting factors in two-stroke engine design these days. As the oil is sprayed, it is also drawn up into the combustion chamber where it forms a carbon deposit on the piston crown and any sharp edges in the cylinder, such as the port rims. This carbon buildup eventually clogs ports and raises the compression ratio of the engine to a point where harmful detonation can occur. Because the heat around the exhaust port is usually the greatest, that is the spot where the greatest carbon buildup will occur and where rather frequent cleaning is needed to keep your chain saw operating most efficiently.

CARBURETION

The carburetor theoretically has the simplest function of all the various engine components. It is required only to atomize the fuel, mix it with air, then pass that fuel/air mixture through the reed or rotary valve into the crankcase where the really complex work goes on.

Carburetor design is based on the venturi principle, which states that a gas or liquid flowing through a bottle neck area in a passage will undergo an increase in speed.

That all sounds simple enough, but in practice the carburetor is one area where major compromises must be made to keep an engine running as well as possible, at as many speeds as possible. There are too many variables to achieve proper carburetion at *all* speeds. First, there's the variable of fuel-to-air ratio by weight. At idle, an engine may need 1 unit of fuel for every 10 or so units of air. At full load the same engine, for top power and good clean running, will need 1 unit of fuel for every 12 or more units of air. And to make things worse, a carburetor will have to supply a fuel/air ratio as low as 1 to 6, for starting in extremely cold weather, to a 1 to 9 ratio for warm weather starting. All these differing fuel ratio needs add complexity in the form of metering circuits, choke levers, and valving.

The carburetor must also maintain a supply of fuel large enough to meet immediate demands for full or part throttle. And it must maintain that supply in a manner that keeps the engine from being choked from fuel overload if the demand suddenly ceases. The schematic of a simple carburetor in Fig. 2-1 shows the basic elements for nearly all chain saw applications.

Figure 2-2 illustrates the operation of the idle and main needles at different throttle openings for a slightly more complex carburetor. In most cases, the single-barrel carburetors, even with the internal fuel pumps and all-position capability found in most modern chain saws, retain a great deal of their simplicity. The four drawings indicate the actions which take place during cold start, idle, part throttle, and high speed.

The exploded drawings of the carburetors from Homelite's 150 AO and 350 Automatic (Fig. 2-3 and 2-4) show units of slightly more complexity and show the units as you would see them in disassembly.

IGNITION

Flywheel magneto is the type of ignition used on all gasoline chain saws (Fig. 2-5). Covering the science of magnetism, or that of electricity, is well beyond the scope of this book, but a quick look at the basics of magneto operation

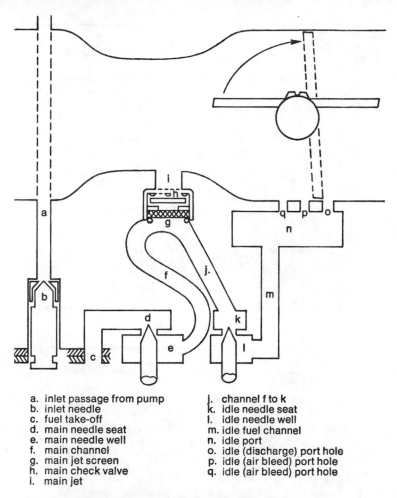

a. inlet passage from pump
b. inlet needle
c. fuel take-off
d. main needle seat
e. main needle well
f. main channel
g. main jet screen
h. main check valve
i. main jet

j. channel f to k
k. idle needle seat
l. idle needle well
m. idle fuel channel
n. idle port
o. idle (discharge) port hole
p. idle (air bleed) port hole
q. idle (air bleed) port hole

Fig. 2-1. A simple chain saw carburetor. (Courtesy Homelite.)

and ignition theory may be a help later when the time arrives to ferret out troubles after a breakdown.

Basically, magnetic field theory states that when a conductor is moved through a magnetic field and cuts *across* the lines of magnetic force, a voltage is induced in the conductor. If the conductor is part of a complete electrical circuit, current will flow through the circuit. Either the magnetic source or the conductor can be moved to induce voltage. An increase in the magnetic field, or in the speed of the conductor as it passes through that field, or an increase in

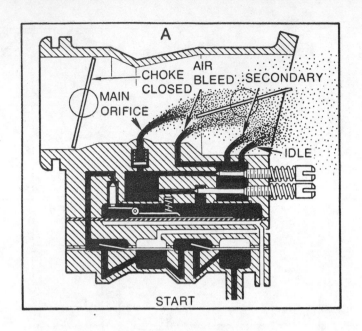

A

CHOKE CLOSED

AIR BLEED

SECONDARY

MAIN ORIFICE

IDLE

START

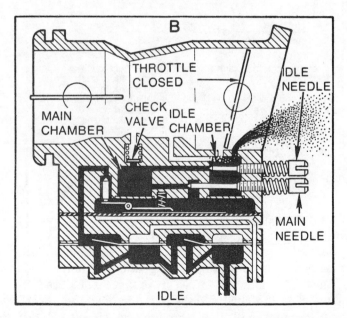

B

THROTTLE CLOSED

IDLE NEEDLE

MAIN CHAMBER

CHECK VALVE

IDLE CHAMBER

MAIN NEEDLE

IDLE

the velocity of the magnetic field will contribute to a greater voltage. An increase in the number of conductors will also increase the voltage generater. Computing the voltage in a

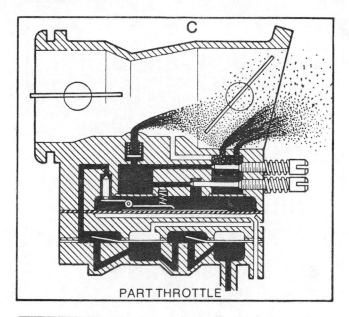

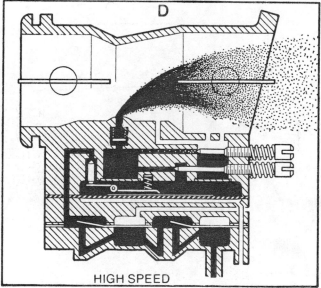

Fig. 2-2. The operation of a diaphragm type carburetor. (Courtesy McCulloch.)

multiconductor generator is simply a matter of multiplying the number of conductors by the voltage produced by a single conductor. Speed of the conductor or magnetic field

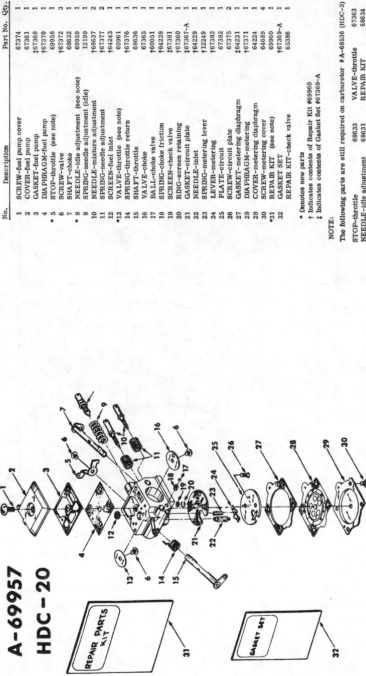

No.	Description	Part No.	Qty.
1	SCREW-fuel pump cover	67374	1
2	COVER-fuel pump	67361	1
3	GASKET-fuel pump	‡67368	1
4	DIAPHRAGM-fuel pump	†67370	1
* 5	STOP-throttle (see note)	69958	1
6	SCREW-valve	67372	3
7	SHAFT-choke	68632	1
* 8	NEEDLE-idle adjustment (see note)	69959	1
9	SPRING-needle adjustment (idle)	12199	1
10	NEEDLE-mixture adjustment	†68637	2
11	SPRING-needle adjustment	†67377	2
12	SCREEN-fuel inlet	†64243	1
*13	VALVE-throttle (see note)	69961	1
14	SPRING-throttle return	†67376	1
15	SHAFT-throttle	68636	1
16	VALVE-choke	67365	1
17	BALL-choke valve	†60051	1
18	SPRING-choke friction	†64238	1
19	SCREEN-check valve	†67381	1
20	RING-screen retaining	†67360	1
21	GASKET-circuit plate	†67367-A	1
22	NEEDLE-inlet	†64229	1
23	SPRING-metering lever	†12249	1
24	LEVER-metering	†67383	1
25	PLATE-circuit	67382	1
26	SCREW-circuit plate	67375	2
27	GASKET-metering diaphragm	†64231	1
28	DIAPHRAGM-metering	†67371	1
29	COVER-metering diaphragm	64224	1
30	SCREW-metering cover	64689	4
*31	REPAIR KIT (see note)	69960	1
32	GASKET SET	†67369-A	1
	REPAIR KIT-check valve	65386	1

NOTE:

The following parts are still required on carburetor #A-68536 (HDC-3)

| STOP-throttle | 68633 | VALVE-throttle | 67363 |
| NEEDLE-idle adjustment | 68631 | REPAIR KIT | 68634 |

* Denotes new parts
† Indicates contents of Repair Kit #69960
‡ Indicates contents of Gasket Set #67369-A

A-69957
HDC-20

REPAIR PARTS KIT — 31

GASKET SET — 32

Fig. 2-3. An exploded view of the carburetor for Homelite's 150 AO.

movement, or the strength of the magnetic field used must, however, remain constant.

Next, let's look at the principle that says whenever an electrical current is flowing through a conductor, there is also a magnetic field around that conductor. The strength of the magnetic field is related to the flow of the current. Therefore, when the rate of flow of the electrical current changes, so too does the strength of the magnetic field.

Thus, flywheel magnets on a magneto ignition are either attached too, or imbedded in, the flywheel itself. To construct a magneto, an armature core is built up of thin plates of soft iron. A high-tension coil consisting of some 100 to 200 windings of medium-weight copper wire and as many as 10,000 windings of finer copper wire (the primary and secondary windings) is wound and placed on the core.

Breaker contact points are installed between the lead from the primary coil winding and ground. The breaker points are opened and closed by a small cam, usually located on the end of the engine crankshaft. A condenser is connected across the points. One job it performs is the reduction of arcing across the points. It functions as the electrical equivalent of an inertial filter by resisting a sudden buildup of energy.

Since the magneto is either attached to, or part of, the flywheel, the turning of the flywheel provides current flow. The breaker points are mechanically arranged to open—called timing the engine—at the correct time to ignite the fuel/air mixture for efficient burning.

Solid state ignition systems begin to force us more deeply into theory than is really necessary for the work most people will care to do. When it becomes necessary to worry about gate controlled switches, diodes, bridge rectifiers, transistors, thyristors, zener diodes and such, its probably the best time to remember that solid-state ignition systems not only do *not* use breaker points, but their working components are in a sealed unit which is replaced when it malfunctions. This applies to just about all solid-state ignition systems, no matter the type. The basic advantages of solid state ignition systems are longer spark plug life, elimination of wear-prone mechanical parts, simplified tuneup procedures (there are, after all, no points to be adjusted or changed), reduced pollutant emissions, and a general reduction of performance degradation between tuneups.

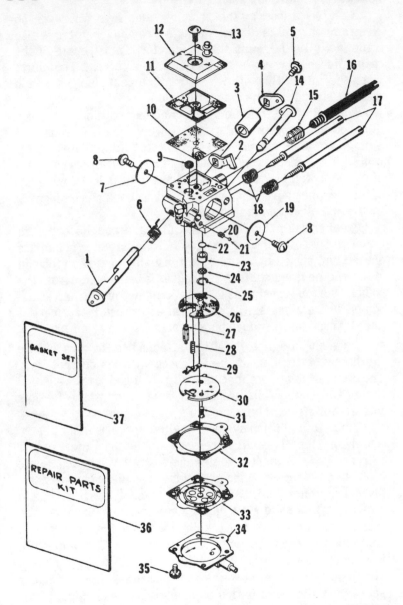

Fig. 2-4. An exploded view of the carburetor on Homelite's 350 automatics.

No.	Description	Qty.
*	KIT – throttle shaft	1
	Includes:	
* 1	SHAFT – throttle	1
* 2	STOP – throttle	1
* 3	SPACER – throttle	1
* 4	LEVER – throttle	1
5	SCREW – valve	1
6	SPRING – throttle return	1
7	VALVE – throttle	1
8	SCREW – valve	2
9	SCREEN – fuel inlet	1
10	DIAPHRAGM – fuel pump	1
11	GASKET – fuel pump	1
12	COVER – fuel pump	1
13	SCREW – pump cover	1
14	SHAFT – choke	1
15	SPRING – idle adjustment	1
16	SCREW – idle adjustment	1
17	NEEDLE – idle adjustment	2
18	SPRING – needle adjustment	2
19	VALVE – choke	1
20	SPRING – choke friction	1
21	BALL – choke friction	1
	REPAIR KIT – check valve (accessory)	1
22	Includes: VALVE – check	1
23	SEAT – valve	1
24	SCREEN – check valve	1
25	RING – screen retaining	1
* 26	GASKET – circuit	1
27	NEEDLE – inlet	1
28	SPRING – metering lever	1
29	LEVER – metering	1
30	PLATE – circuit (HDC-16)	1
*	PLATE – circuit (HDC-21)	1
31	SCREW – circuit plate	2
32	GASKET – metering diaphragm	1
33	DIAPHRAGM – metering	1
34	COVER – metering diaphragm	1
35	SCREW – metering cover	4
* 36	REPAIR KIT	1
* 37	GASKET SET	1
*	KIT – high altitude (accessory)	1
	Includes: PLATE – circuit	1
*	GASKET – circuit	1
*	LABEL	1

* Denotes new parts

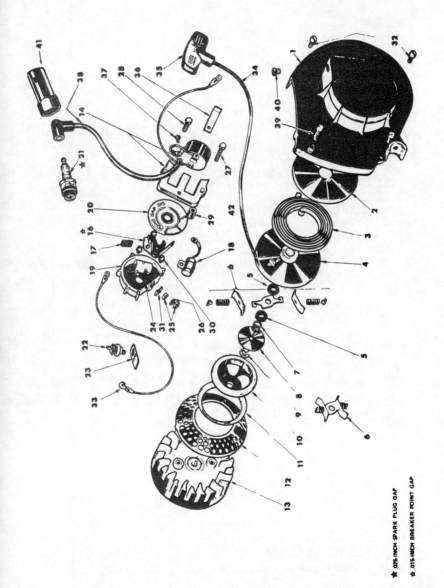

★ .025-INCH SPARK PLUG GAP

☆ .015-INCH BREAKER POINT GAP

40

REF. NO.	PART NO.	DESCRIPTION
1	178674	FAN HOUSING & STARTER ASSEMBLY (including STARTER)
2	178675	FAN & STARTER HOUSING ASSEMBLY
3	178287	SPRING RETAINER
4	178317	SPRING
5	178297	ROTOR
6	178100	FIBRE WASHER (2 used)
7	178676	FRICTION SHOE ASSEMBLY
8	178319	BRAKE SPRING
9	178323	BRAKE RETAINING WASHER
10	178324	"E" CLIP
11	178126	STARTER CUP
12	178128	STARTER SNOW SHIELD
13	178127	STARTER SCREEN
14	178658	FLYWHEEL
15	178685	COIL and CORE ASSEMBLY
16	178663	BREAKER ASSEMBLY
17	178452	CAM WIPER FELT
18	178664	CONDENSER
19	178450	CONTACT BREAKER HOUSING
20	178451	BREAKER HOUSING COVER
21	270523	SPARK PLUG J.6J.

REF. NO.	PART NO.	DESCRIPTION
22	270238	SWITCH
23	183269	SWITCH PLATE
24	178163	SCREW
25	850008	NUT (2 used)
26	44572	SPRING LOCK WASHER
27	707210	COIL MOUNTING SCREW - LONG
28	706410	COIL MOUNTING SCREW - SHORT
29	178144	COIL SCREW SPACER
30	735508	FIXED CONTACT CLAMP SCREW (3 used)
31	178453	CHANNEL WASHER
32	726010	FAN HOUSING MOUNTING SCREW (3 used)
33	178087	STOP SWITCH LEAD
34	178600	STARTER CORD ASSEMBLY
35	178639	TEE HANDLE ASSEMBLY
36	178147	COIL CLIP
37	178148	COIL CLIP SCREW
38	178666	HIGH TENSION LEAD ASSEMBLY
39	726810	FAN HOUSING MOUNTING SCREW
40	178327	BUSHING
41	270522	PLUG WRENCH
43	179076	RETAINER

Fig. 2-5. A typical magneto and starter.

Spark plugs require more care from the chain saw owner. A good spark plug, of correct heat range and proper gap, is an essential element in getting an internal combustion, reciprocating, nondiesel engine to run and continue running at maximum efficiency. The spark plug provides a means for igniting the fuel/air mixture. That's not just the spark plug's primary job, it's the plug's *only* job. Any other spark plug features, such as heat transfer, are used only to aid in getting the correct spark at the correct time. A clean, correctly gapped plug may require as little as 7000 volts to ignite a fuel/air mixture. A dirty, fouled, improperly gapped plug may

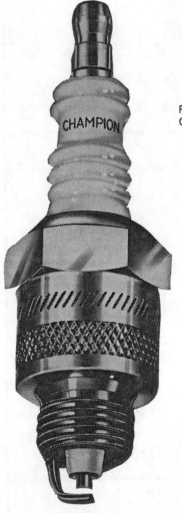

Fig. 2-6. Spark plug. (Courtesy Champion Spark Plug Co.)

not fire the mixture no matter how much voltage is used. Tight gaps can cut down a bit on the needed voltage; they can also cause many problems such as premature plug fouling and preignition. Also, as the top of the piston becomes carbonized, the voltage needs of the spark plug increase, for the effective compression ratio of the engine increases.

Selecting the proper spark plug, gapping it correctly, and making sure it doesn't foul will do more for your chain saw engine than any other single maintenance chore (if the saw is in basically good condition).

A spark plug is shown in Fig. 2-6. Spark plugs have three important characteristics.

Thread size. The threaded base of the spark plug and the spark plug hole in the cylinder must be the same size. Normal spark plug thread sizes are 10 millimeters (mm), 14 mm, and 18 mm. Nearly every chain saw made today uses 14 mm spark plugs.

Reach. The depth to which the plug thread reaches into the cylinder is called reach. With too long a reach the plug nose can hit the crown of the piston. Too short a reach means the plug won't fire in the cylinder but will fire inside its own little chamber. Chain saws commonly use 3/8 or 7/16 inch reach spark plugs.

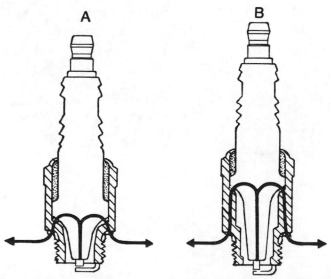

Fig. 2-7. Spark plug heat ranges: cold range (A), hot range (B). (Courtesy Champion Spark Plug Co.)

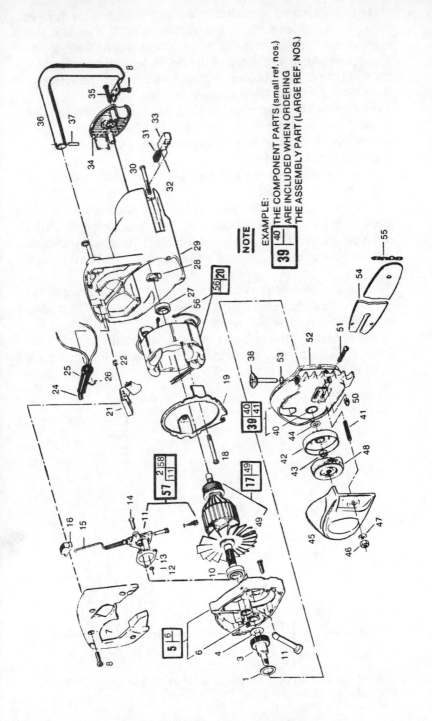

NOTE

EXAMPLE:

$\dfrac{39}{40}$ THE COMPONENT PARTS (small ref. nos.) ARE INCLUDED WHEN ORDERING THE ASSEMBLY PART (LARGE REF. NOS.)

44

REF. NO.	PART NAME
1	WASHER...AS REQ.
2	OIL FILTER
3	GEAR SPINDLE
4	WASHER
5	BEARING PLATE ASSEMBLY
6	BEARING
7	HANDLE COVER
8	SCREW
9	SCREW
10	BALL BEARING
11	OIL PUMP
12	"O"RING
13	PUMP GASKET
14	SCREW
15	PUMP ROD
16	OILER BUTTON
17	ARMATURE (115 V.)
18	SCREW
19	BAFFLE
20	FIELD (115 V.)
21	SWITCH...)
22	WASHER...)
23	SAFETY SWITCH BUTTON
24	CORD & CAP

REF. NO.	PART NAME
25	CORD GUARD
26	CORD CLAMP
27	BALL BEARING
28	SPRING LOADING WASHER
29	MOTOR HOUSING
30	SCREW
31	BRUSH
32	BRUSH SPRING
33	BRUSH HOLDER
34	END COVER
35	SCREW
36	HANDLE
37	HANDLE PIN
38	OIL LEVEL INDICATOR
39	GEAR HOUSING ASSEMBLY
40	BEARING
41	STUD...)
42	SPROCKET & DRUM
43	BEARING
44	WASHER
45	CLUTCH COVER
46	NUT
47	FLAT WASHER
48	CLUTCH

REF. NO.	PART NAME
49	FAN
50	BAR ADJUSTER NUT
51	SCREW
52	GASKET
53	GASKET
54	GUIDE BAR
55	CHAIN
56	TERMINAL
57	OIL PUMP & FILTER ASSEM.
58	TUBING

Fig. 2-8. Skil 1602 Type 1 electric chain saw engine.

Heat Range. The operating temperature of the spark plug is important to overall engine operation. If the plug retains too much heat, preignition may occur as the fuel/air mixture is ignited prematurely. It's a good way to ruin any engine if it occurs too often. If not enough heat is retained, the plug will quickly foul with the partially burned products of combustion, such as soot and oil (Fig. 2-7).

ELECTRIC MOTORS

Electric motors on chain saws are the universal type. Universal electric motors (Fig. 2-8) provide a lot of power over a wide speed range and thus, are better suited to chain saw application than the shaded pole motors most often found in small fans and hair driers. The universal motor is so named because it can usually be used, with equal results, on alternating current (AC) or direct current (DC).

Electric motor theory takes us right back to electromagnetic theory. In this case, though, electricity is used to drive the device, rather than being the energy generated. This is done by forcing the north and south poles of magnetic field(s) within the motor to change as the rotor turns. Of course, *like* poles repel, *unlike* poles attract, so as the poles change they are kept in a continual state of repellence/attraction, thus spinning the shaft of the motor which carries the drive sprocket for the chain saw.

Within the motor, stationary field coils surround an armature. The shaft holding the armature has a commutator made of copper plates on a thickened portion of that shaft. Carbon brushes ride gently against the multielement commutator which is electrically connected to armature coils. Specifically, each element of the commutator is electrically attached to its adjacent coil. The brushes transmit electrical power to the commutator which passes it to armature coils on opposite sides of the armature. This is a consecutive action, for as the commutator turns, the two brushes make sequential contact with each commutator plate. This action creates a varying series of north and south magnetic poles which literally forces the motor to turn. This provides the rotary power required to pull a chain around the guide bar.

Should a universal motor fail in an electric chain saw, there's not a lot you can do except replace it, unless you have a home shop equipped with coil winding equipment and a fair amount of electrical test gear. General saw maintenance usually involves little more than occasional brush replacement and lubrication.

Occasional insulation breakdowns resulting in short circuits can also be corrected if they can be traced (but again it is a job for fairly specialized equipment). In most cases, insulation breakdowns are a sign of either excessive motor overheating or factory defects.

Other than that, there just isn't much to adjust or go wrong with an electric chain saw. It either works or it doesn't. If the chain saw quits, you need only to discover whether it's a short circuit, an open circuit, or a beat up and worn out motor. If the short or open is accessible in a wire or switch assembly, it can usually be corrected. If the short or open is internal, in the field coils, for example, you'll nearly always have to replace the entire motor. That simplicity is the very reason the section on electric chains saws is the shortest in this book.

Chapter 3
Basic Chain Saw Care

Basic Chain Saw Care

Any tool, whether it's a chain saw or a carpenter's plane, will last longer and operate more efficiently if it receives proper day-to-day care and feeding. No one can deny that a lot of progress has been made in many fields, so very basic maintenance is not now needed quite as frequently as in earlier years. Better oil and grease provide simpler, longer lasting lubrication. Better metals and metal coating methods—nearly all homeowner's chain saws have chrome plated cylinder bores now—provide longer life even under the most extreme conditions. But no matter what the quality, it's still possible to misuse the finest piece of machinery in the world and ruin it in just a few minutes or hours of operation. Minimal care will provide minimal tool life. With correct handling and care, that same piece of machinery will efficiently cycle through its design life.

FUEL

Correct fuel mixture will contribute greatly to engine running life. It will also make a major contribution to clean running and long spark plug life. Each depends largely on the type of oil used when mixing the fuel. Nearly as much can depend on the fuel container used.

First, select a clean fuel container. The fuel container should always be a heavy safety can with venting. Unvented fuel cans always present those who use them with surprises because gasoline is highly volatile—even a slight temperature change causes it to expand or contract a great deal in volume. Thus an unvented can, no matter how heavy, will often leak. Or it will, if light enough in weight, bulge and finally rupture a seam.

Next, select the gasoline to be used. The fuel must be clean and fresh. See Fig. 3-1 for details of fuel life. Almost all chain saws operate perfectly well on regular grade gasoline of 90 octane or more. Experience will help you decide how much to mix for a day's running, but mix only a large enough amount of gasoline to last two or three days. Gasoline stored much longer than that will lose some of the higher, more volatile fractions that make an engine easy to start. Add to this the strong probability that air will enter the fuel container and that the air will condense. The fuel, then watered out, can clog the fuel filter, reducing the flow of fuel to the carburetor. This cuts engine speed in proportion to just how badly the filter becomes clogged.

Never store a chain saw with a full fuel tank. First, there's always the danger of fire from improperly stored volatile liquids. Second, the fuel becomes stale as the saw sits without being used. If you use your chain saw only every few months, stale fuel, at best, will cause the saw to become hard starting. At worst, the saw won't start at all because the fuel has lost high fraction volatiles essential to efficient combustion. If your saw is to be stored for more than a week or two, remove all fuel in the tank: turn it upside down over a pan and let the tank drain. When getting ready to start the saw a couple of months later, add a few ounces of fresh fuel, swish it around, and pour it out. This will take out most of the fuel residues. Refill with a fresh fuel/oil mixture and start.

OIL

The oil added to your chain saw's gasoline should be of a type designed specifically for use with two stroke engines. Avoid all multigrade and other products designed for four-stroke engines; they will not mix properly with gas and often do not even come close to having the correct additives to provide the needed protection for your saw's internal parts. Four-stroke oil, too, is usually a lot harder on two-stroke spark plugs, causing a great deal of fouling.

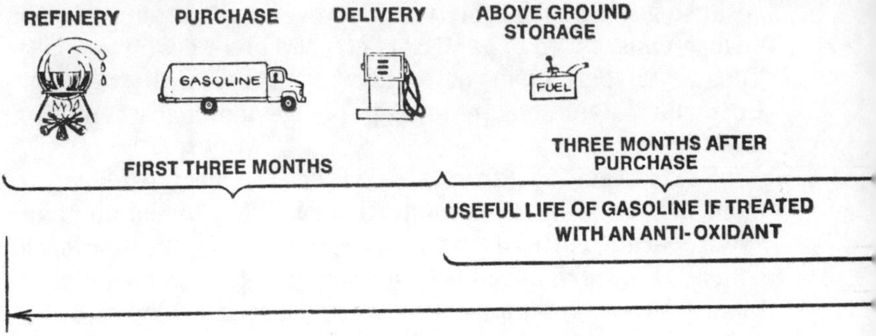

REFINERY   PURCHASE   DELIVERY   ABOVE GROUND STORAGE

GASOLINE

FUEL

FIRST THREE MONTHS

THREE MONTHS AFTER PURCHASE

USEFUL LIFE OF GASOLINE IF TREATED WITH AN ANTI-OXIDANT

Fig. 3-1. The useful life of gasoline if treated with an anti-oxidant is 6 months. Untreated gasoline is good for three months. (Courtesy Homelite.)

Gasoline and oil should be mixed in amounts recommended by the manufacturer of the *oil*. If the oil container calls for a mixture of 1 part oil to 32 parts gasoline, that's the best way to use it. If you're using a borderline product—something to be avoided unless you absolutely have to use your chain saw and no other oil is available—such as snowmobile or outboard motor oil, a mix of 16 to 1 should prevent excess engine wear. There are, also, two-stroke oils that recommend mixing at 40 to 1, and a few that will do the job when mixed at 50 to 1. My own personal preference has for years been a two-stroke motorcycle racing oil called Full Bore. It is mixed at 32 to 1 (an ounce of the oil to a quart of gasoline). It has never fouled a spark plug, and I've never had internal engine damage attributable to the oil.

There are now a very large number of fine two-stroke oils on the market, including those sold by various chain saw manufacturers. Select one that will do the best job for you, but don't be swayed even a little bit by the cost of the oil. At 32 to 1, a single quart of two-stroke motor oil will mix with 32 quarts (8 gallons) of gasoline. Eight gallons of gasoline is going to run any chain saw for an awfully long time, so the difference between $1.50 per quart and $2.50 per quart means very little.

Measurement of oil and gasoline for mixing can be a problem for some people, but it really shouldn't cause any difficulty. Fill the mixing container half full, then pour in the correct amount of oil. Agitate vigorously. Now, pour in the rest of the gas and stir or shake for a minute or so. To measure the oil, I use plastic baby bottles that come with ounce markings on the side. A measuring cup would also be a good idea, but the

52

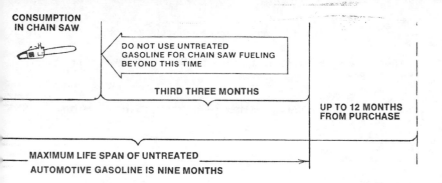

CONSUMPTION
IN CHAIN SAW

DO NOT USE UNTREATED
GASOLINE FOR CHAIN SAW FUELING
BEYOND THIS TIME

THIRD THREE MONTHS

UP TO 12 MONTHS
FROM PURCHASE

MAXIMUM LIFE SPAN OF UNTREATED
AUTOMOTIVE GASOLINE IS NINE MONTHS

baby bottles allow you to easily store 8 ounces or so of oil, tightly capped.

Never pour unmixed oil or gasoline directly into the chain saw's gas tank. With the small amount these tanks hold, precise measurement is difficult; making sure it is well mixed requires a lot of saw shaking.

Remove the fuel cap and fill the tank. Wipe off any fuel spilled on the saw. Make sure the cap is tightened when it's replaced (chainsaws vibrate a lot, so any little bit of fuel cap looseness can cause the thing to chatter right off the saw, spilling gas all over the place).

FILTERS

Air filtration is one aspect of chain saw care that is too often ignored or put off for longer than the manufacturer recommends. The air filter on almost all modern chain saws is accessible by removing a single nut, screw, or fastener (Fig. 3-2). It should be cleaned at least twice during every operating day of eight hours or more. In most cases, all you need do is remove the filter cover, remove the filter element, and either wipe it off or tap it lightly on a hard surface. Then cover the carburetor air intake tube and wipe the surrounding surfaces clean of grit and dust. Naturally, if cutting conditions are exceptionally dusty, you'll need to clean the filter more frequently. Some air filters are washable and should be soaked in detergent and then rinsed thoroughly and allowed to air dry completely before reinstallation. It's always a good idea to carry a couple of extra filters with you into the woods or other work area so you won't have to worry about dusty or other poor cutting conditions. See Table 3-1 for maintenance schedule.

Table 3-1. Maintenance Schedule

The following maintenance schedule applies to all makes of chain saws.

Job	Daily	5 Hrs.	15 Hrs.	25 Hrs.	50 Hrs.
Examine saw exterior for cracks and flaws.	X				
Clean saw and guide bar with a dry rag.	X				
Reverse guide bar to equalize wear top and bottom.		X			
Remove and clean guide bar, mounting pad area, and oil discharge hole.		X			
Check air filter for cleanliness.		X			
Check muffler for carbon clogging. Clean out any clogging.		X			
Lower chain depth gauges.		X			
Sharpen chain.		X			
Check fuel filter.			X		
Disassemble muffler; clean muffler and cylinder exhaust port.				X	
Clean and regap spark plug.					X
Clean cylinder fins, air intake, and all engine cooling passageways.			X		

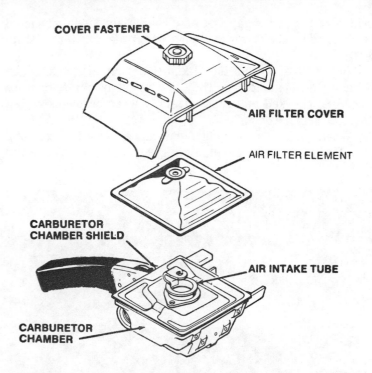

COVER FASTENER

AIR FILTER COVER

AIR FILTER ELEMENT

CARBURETOR
CHAMBER SHIELD

AIR INTAKE TUBE

CARBURETOR
CHAMBER

Fig. 3-2. Getting to a chain saw air filter is usually just a matter of removing a single nut. (Courtesy Homelite.)

When reinstalling air filters, make certain they fit the air chamber edges closely. If the filter has been bent, it probably won't fit properly; discard it and use a new filter. Never operate a chain saw engine without an air filter. Incidentally, a dirty air filter cuts down on air intake capability and results in overrich carburetion, which cuts way down on power.

You can also do the following for even better filtering. A coating of medium weight white grease in the air filter box will trap dirt particles. This coating should be light, almost invisible, and should be wiped off and renewed every time the air filter is cleaned.

SPARK PLUGS

Spark plug maintenance is a very simple job. Even on a new saw, the spark plug should be removed and checked for correct gapping and heat range. Even the best manufacturers sometimes goof, especially when a production line is running several shifts a day at full capacity. On older saws, when the plug is removed for gapping or cleaning, its condition should be checked by eye or with a plug scope if one is available (Fig. 3-3).

Check Figs. 3-4 to 3-10 to identify engine problems. Learn to read your spark plugs. They are an engine's tattletale and should be checked and read carefully when problems with a chain saw engine occur.

When gapping spark plugs, use only a round wire gapping tool. Those flat metal gapping gauges do not give an accurate

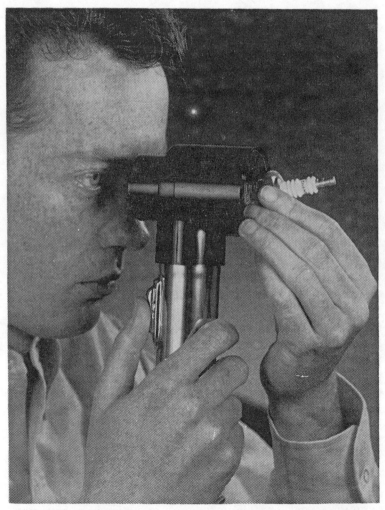

Fig. 3-3. Using a spark plug scope. (Courtesy Champion Spark Plug Co.)

Fig. 3-4. Normal plug wear. Normal plugs have brown to grayish tan deposits and slight electrode wear, indicating correct spark plug heat range and periods of high and low speed driving. Plugs with normal wear may be cleaned, regapped, and reinstalled. (Courtesy Champion Spark Plug Co.)

Fig. 3-5. Oil fouled spark plug. Wet oily deposits may be caused by too much oil in the fuel mixture. Breakin of a new or overhauled engine before rings are fully seated may also produce oil fouling. Usually oil fouled plugs can be degreased, cleaned, and reinstalled. (Courtesy Champion Spark Plug Co.)

Fig. 3-6. Carbon fouled spark plug. Carbon fouled plugs have dry fluffy black deposits which may be caused by overrich carburetion, overchoking, or a clogged air cleaner. Faulty breaker points, weak coil and condenser, and worn ignition cables can reduce voltage and cause misfiring—which causes carbon fouling. Excessive idling and slow speeds under light loads can also keep plug temperatures so low that normal combustion deposits are not burned off. Low plug temperatures can be remedied with a hotter type spark plug. (Courtesy Champion Spark Plug Co.)

Fig. 3-7. Spark plug with burned electrodes. Burned or blistered insulator nose and badly eroded electrodes are indications of spark plug overheating. Improper spark plug timing or low octane fuel can cause this. Lean air/fuel mixtures and cooling system stoppages may also cause spark plug overheating. Sustained high-speed, heavy-load service can produce high tempertures that require colder spark plugs. (Champion Spark Plug Co.)

Fig. 3-8. Spark plug with reversed electrode bend. The improper use of pliers-type gap setting tools can bend the side electrode. These tools must be used with care. (Champion Spark Plug Co.)

gap indication for spark plugs. Proper spark plug gaps for most chain saws are shown in Table 3-2.

CHAIN AND GUIDE BAR

Always be sure to fill the chain oil reservoir with a good quality oil, either special chain oil or a middle weight motor oil with no additives. An improperly cared for chain, incorrect chain tension, a dull chain, a chain with broken cutters, a guide bar with faults: all of these can make a chain saw engine seem to have problems even when it's in perfect shape. The chain saw engine is specifically designed to pull a cutting chain through the wood when everything in the system is in peak condition.

Fig. 3-9. Spark plug with broken insulator. Fractured insulators can indicate severe detonation. Indiscriminate bending of the center electrode can also cause a cracked insulator. Check for cause of detonation and install new plugs. (Courtesy Champion Spark Plug Co.)

Table 3-2. Tuning Specifications

Saw Model	Spark plug	Point Gap	Plug Gap	Engine size	Ignition timing
Homelite					
EZ	CJ-6J Champion	0.025	0.015	2.1 CID	preset
EZ Auto	CJ-6J Champion	0.025	0.015	2.3 CID	preset
Super EZ	CJ-6J Champion	0.025	0.015	2.5 CID	preset
XL-Mini	CJ-6J Champion	0.025	0.015	2.1 CID	preset
XL-Mini Auto	CJ-6J Champion	0.025	0.015	2.3 CID	preset
KL-12[1]	CJ-6 or CJ-8 Champion	0.025	0.015	3.3 CID	preset
150 Auto	DJ-7J Champion	0.025	0.015	2.64 CID	preset
XL-2	DJ-7J Champion	0.025	0.015	1.6 CID	preset
Jonsenreds					
Lil-Jon 50	CJ-8 Champion	0.025	0.017	2.1 CID	2.0 mm BTDC (0.079 in.)
601	CJ-7Y Champion	0.025	0.015	3.0 CID	3.2 mm DTDC (0.126 in.)
621	CJ-7Y Champion	0.025	0.015	3.0 CID	2.7 mm BTDC (0.106 in.)
Lombard					
Comango	CJ-6J Champion	0.025	0.015	4.2 CID	30 degrees BTDC
Comango Auto	CJ-6J Champion	0.025	0.015	4.2 CID	30 degrees BTDC
Super Comango	CJ-6J Champion	0.025	0.015	4.2 CID	30 degrees BTDC
S.C. Auto	CJ-6J Champion	0.025	0.015	4.2 CID	30 degrees BTDC
McCulloch					
Mini Mac 1	CS45T (AC)	0.025	0.018	1.78 CID	preset
Mac 1 Auto	CS45T (AC)	0.025	0.018	1.78 CID	preset
Mini Mac 6	CS45T (AC)	0.025	0.018	1.78 CID	preset
Power Mac 6	CS45T (AC)	0.025	0.018	2.0 CID	preset
Mac 10-10	CS45T (AC)	0.025	0.017	3.3 CID	preset
Pioneer					
P20	CJ-6 Champion	0.030	0.015	3.14 CID	30 degrees BTDC
P25	CJ-6 Champion	0.030	0.015	3.14 CID	30 degrees BTDC
p40	CJ-8 Champion	0.030	0.015	3.97 CID	30 degrees BTDC
Beaird-Poulan					
25D	CJ-8 Champion	0.025	0.017	2.1 CID	preset
25DA	CJ-8 Champion	0.025	0.017	2.1 CID	preset
306	3014 (Poulan)	0.025	0.020	3.6 CID	preset
306A	3014 (Poulan)	0.025	0.020	3.6 CID	preset
306SA	3014 (Poulan)	0.025	0.020	3.6 CID	preset
245	3014 (Poulan)	0.025	0.020	4.0 CID	preset
245A	3014 (Poulan)	0.025	0.020	4.0 CID	preset
361	3014 (Poulan)	0.025	0.015	3.6 CID	preset
Remington					
Mighty Mite	CJ-6 Champion	0.025	0.015	2.1 CID	preset
MM Auto	CJ-6 Champion	0.025	0.015	2.1 CID	preset
SL-9	CJ-6 Champion	0.025	0.015	2.8 CID	preset
SL-10	CJ-6 Champion	0.025	0.015	3.1 CID	preset
SL-11	CJ-6 Champion	0.025	0.015	4.0 CID	preset
Roper					
C11031R	DJ-6J Champion	0.025	0.015	1.9 CID	preset
C12131R	DJ-6J Champion	0.025	0.015	1.9 CID	preset
C33231R	CJ-6 Champion	0.025	0.015	3.7 CID	preset
C34331R	CJ-6 Champion	0.025	0.015	3.7 CID	preset
C35431R	CJ-6 Champion	0.025	0.015	3.7 CID	preset
Sears[2]					
Skil					
1630	J-6J Champion	0.025	0.015	4.2 CID	preset
1631	J-6J Champion	0.025	0.015	4.2 CID	preset
Solo					
610	WKA-175 T6 (Bosch)	0.020	0.014-0.017	1.98 CID	preset
615	WKA-175 (Bosch)	0.020	0.014-0.017	2.745 CID	preset
600	WKA-175 (Bosch)	0.020	0.014-0.016	1.95 CID	preset
Stihl					
020AV	WKA-175 T6 (Bosch)	0.020	0.014-0.016	1.96 CID	0.08-0.087 BTDC
030AV	WKA-175 T6 (Bosch)	0.020	0.014-0.016	2.7 CID	0.08-0.087 BTDC
031AV	WKA-175 T6 (Bosch)	0.020	0.014-0.016	3.2 CID	0.08-0.087 BTDC
041AV	WKA-175 T6 (Bosch)	0.020	0.014-0.016	3.72 CID	0.098-0.102 BTDC
	WKA-175 T6 (Bosch)	0.025			

[1] Spark plug terminals on the XL-12 may have to be changed to allow earlier models to use the CJ series spark plugs.

[2] At one time or another, Sears has sold saws with engines for Roper, Poulan, and Tecumseh. For the specifications on your particular saw, take the model number to your local Sears store and have them look up the information or supply you with a factory manual.

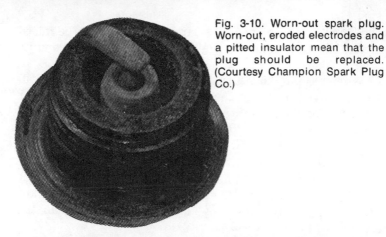

Fig. 3-10. Worn-out spark plug. Worn-out, eroded electrodes and a pitted insulator mean that the plug should be replaced. (Courtesy Champion Spark Plug Co.)

Chain tension is probably a specification most new chain saw operators overlook during maintenance. First, though, before checking the tension, make certain your hands are protected. You can either use a rag to hold the chain or wear heavy gloves as you check the tension and tighten things up. Cutters on a good chain are very sharp.

Two important steps must be taken before you adjust chain tension on a guide bar. First, the nose of the bar must be held in an upward position as the bar mounting nuts, bolts, and screws are loosened (Fig. 3-11). Next, it is necessary to pull the chain along the guide bar until it reaches a point of maximum tension. When the drive sprocket turns, the tautness of the chain will vary. A chain that has been tightened at a "loose" spot will be too tight when the chain saw is in operation. During operation a warm chain usually will loosen up a bit, but the still over-tight chain creates drag, which

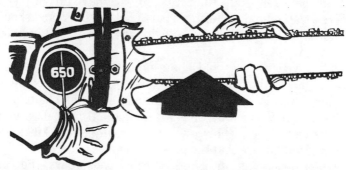

Fig. 3-11. Hold the bar upward during the entire tensioning procedure. (Courtesy Homelite.)

reduces cutting efficiency. The bar nose must always be raised since such action takes up any play between the bar and its mounting bolts.

With the bar mounting nuts finger tight, and nearly all slack removed from the chain, lift the nose of the guide bar and move the chain until you're sure it's at that one point of maximum tautness. When you first start making chain adjustments, this step will probably take you several tries.

If the guide bar is of the hard nose variety, set the tension, when cold, so that the chain tie straps at the center of the lower chain span do not quite touch the bar rails. The tie straps should hang away from the guide bar no more than the thickness of a dime (Fig. 3-12)

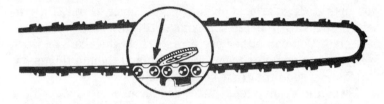

Fig. 3-12. Tension setting for a hard nose bar (cold. (Courtesy Homelite.)

To adjust a warm chain on a hard nose guide bar, set the chain to the point where the tangs hang about half way out of the bar's groove at the center of the lower span. This will leave about an inch between the chain's tie straps and the guide bar rails. A warm chain should not need adjustment until the drive tangs hang all the way out of the guide bar grooves. Do not adjust if the chain is overheated. Check by holding the nose of the bar between your fingertips, if you have to pull your fingers away quickly, the chain is too hot to adjust and should be allowed to cool until it can be held for a few seconds without discomfort.

When you have a cold chain on a hard nose guide bar, always check the tension before going to the trouble of loosening and retensioning. Before tightening the chain, snap the chain a few times by lifting it up and letting it drop back onto the bar. This snapping will remove any minor kinks and binds and will insure that the tensioning job is accurate.

When tensioning sprocket, or roller, nose bars, the cold tension should be snug, as shown in Fig. 3-13. If the chain moves freely around the guide bar but is good and tight otherwise, the tension is just fine. The chain will expand as the saw cuts, but the cooling down process will find the chain retracting nearly to its original setting. Under very heavy cutting conditions, the chain on a sprocket nose guide bar may sag to the point where no more than the tips of the drive tangs remain in the guide bar groove. If they move out further than that, and additional heavy duty cutting is on tap, readjust the warm, not hot, bar and chain. The adjustment should be made so that about half the depth of the chain drive tangs is visible at the center of the chain span. Incidentally, if this warm adjustment is made, the chain will almost certainly be too tight when it cools down. You must readjust the bar and chain to its correct cold tension.

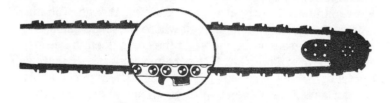

Fig. 3-13. Tension setting for a roller nose bar (cold). (Courtesy Homelite.)

No matter what kind of guide bar you use, the nose of the bar must be held up throughout the tensioning procedure. In fact, it must be held up until the guide bar mounting bolts are finally tightened.

For all types of bars, the chain must be moved by hand after the guide bar mounting bolts have been tightened in order to check for binding caused by overtension or some other problems, such as guide bar burring. As long as the chain can easily be moved around the guide bar by hand, there should be no problem.

Don't get overly eager to make chain adjustments. A new chain will probably require adjustment after an hour or so of running time, but a used chain under normal use should hold its shape for quite some time. Since so much depends on your cutting style, the type of wood, the seasoning of the wood, the air temperature, chain adjustment intervals are hard to fix. There's really no need to readjust the chain until the drive tangs drop that final fraction of an inch out of the guide bar groove. If it happens with a warm bar, adjust!

Too tight a chain will increase friction which in turn, heats the guide bar and chain. Too much heat can ruin the temper of the guide bar where the chain binds (it will also ruin the chain, another unneeded expense). If it happens, you'll see indications of overheating by looking for a spot on the guide bar.

Sometimes, though, the problem is not brought on by poor adjustment. Since guide bars can and often do receive rough treatment, they can become burred and pinched. So, if the chain tension is correct, and the guide bar still shows signs of overheating, then the guide bar is probably pinching the chain's drive tangs and must be bent away at that spot. To make the adjustment, use a screwdriver of appropriate size—a little smaller than the guide bar groove—and gently pry the side rails apart a little at a time. Careful, though. Too much force can open the rails to a point where the chain "slops" and "slaps" dangerously. Of course, if the chain itself is oversized, the guide bar will pinch it. If the chain is undersized, there will be a lot of "play." The only cure is a new chain of correct size for your saw. Check the chapter on chains and guide bars for more details on chain and guide bar problems and repairs.

The guide bar will have one or more holes at the start of the chain groove. These holes are chain oil passages. They are there so the oil can be transported to the chain to help cut down on wear and tear (Fig. 3-14). After each day's cutting, the chain should be removed from the bar. The bar should then be removed from the powerhead so the oil holes and groove can be checked for sawdust and grit accumulation. Use a stiff wire to clean out the oil holes and drive tang groove (the drive tangs normally keep the groove clean, but the oil hole can clog easily). Too little oil will result in hard cutting. But if oil starvation is really severe, the guide bar will start to heat and discolor, usually near the tip where strains are greatest.

Chain oil should be checked each time the fuel level is checked—more often if you're doing a lot of cutting in seasoned hardwood or exceptionally resinous woods. On saws offering both an automatic and manual oiler, chain oil level will drop rapidly in heavy duty use, so the reservoir must be checked quite frequently.

Chain oil is formulated specially by companies making chain saws. But if you can't locate chain oil, any good quality 30 weight motor oil will do a fair job in moderate weather. If

64

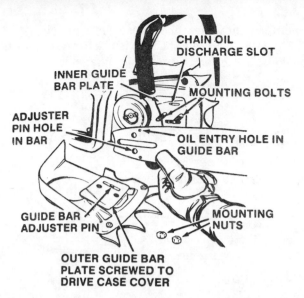

CHAIN OIL DISCHARGE SLOT

INNER GUIDE BAR PLATE

MOUNTING BOLTS

ADJUSTER PIN HOLE IN BAR

OIL ENTRY HOLE IN GUIDE BAR

GUIDE BAR ADJUSTER PIN

MOUNTING NUTS

OUTER GUIDE BAR PLATE SCREWED TO DRIVE CASE COVER

Fig. 3-14. Oil discharge slot and oil entry hole on a chain saw. (Courtesy Homelite.)

the weather becomes exceptionally cold, you will require a lighter viscosity oil flow to meet demand. Either the oil in use can be thinned slightly with kerosene, or you can make a switch to SAE 10 or 20 weight oil (depending on actual weather severity). Never use multiviscosity oils for chain oiling. These oils have a lot of unnecessary additives.

To check chain oil flow, first let the saw idle until the engine is warmed up. Then hold the tip of the guide bar about a foot away from a clean piece of wood and speed up the engine. If the oiler is filled and working, the chain should throw a moderate spray of oil onto the wood surface. If it doesn't, first check the chain oil reservoir. Next check the weather. If the temperature is under 35 degrees, you'll probably have to use thinner chain oil. If that still doesn't help, check the oil holes in the powerhead and the guide bar. If they are clean, either the pump is faulty or the filter is clogged. Repairs are going to be needed. See the chapter on overhauls.

Roller nose guide bars need lubrication with a special grease gun. At the end of each day's operation (more often under heavy duty cutting) the guide bar should be wiped clean of sawdust. Then while the guide bar is still warm, the grease gun should be placed on the special nozzle holes in the bar and grease pumped into the roller nose until all old grease is purged (Fig. 3-15). The saw should then be flipped over and the same job done, in the same way, to the other side.

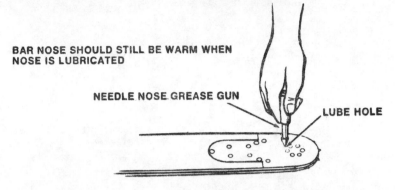

BAR NOSE SHOULD STILL BE WARM WHEN NOSE IS LUBRICATED

NEEDLE NOSE GREASE GUN

LUBE HOLE

Fig. 3-15. Lubricating a roller nose guide bar.(Courtesy Homelite.)

A sprocket noise guide bar lubricated before it is warmed may not have all the old grease forced out. Forcing out old grease also pushes out all the old sawdust and grit.

Sprocket noise bearings are good as long as they can be turned freely by hand without roughness or binding. The nose is easily replaced when the time comes for a new one.

ENGINE TUNING

Proper engine tuning can keep any chain saw operating at top power for a longer period of time. Two-stroke engines require particular attention to several things not normally considered when tuning four-stroke engines, such as cleaning exhaust ports and the muffler. A basic tuneup requires a new spark plug, new magneto breaker points, timing, a carburetor adjustment, exhaust port, muffler, and engine cooling fin cleaning.

Spark Plug

For a saw that gets light use, the most sensible spot to start is with a spark plug change. Frequently a new spark plug will make a small engine run as though it just had a complete tuneup. In such cases, it doesn't really pay to replace and set the points (though it may well pay to make sure the cooling fins, exhaust port, and muffler are clean).

Magneto System

To check the magneto system including the breaker points, remove the spark plug and check it against the spark plug photos presented earlier in this chapter. Take the spark plug boot and slip a metal rod about 1/4 inch in diameter into it so that the rod contacts the spring connector inside the boot. Grasp the spark plug boot well back on the insulator and hold the rod about 1/4 inch away from a metal part of the engine. The distance between the rod and the metal is called the air gap. Turn the ignition switch *on*. Crank the engine as though you were trying to start it. If a bright blue spark jumps the air gap, there's no need to replace the breaker points (Fig. 3-16). Your magneto and the points are both doing a fine job. When you are outside, the sun is sometimes too bright for you to see this spark. In this case, just listen for a sharp snapping noise. That snap indicates a good, strong spark.

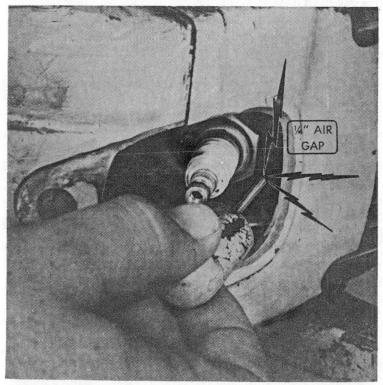

Fig. 3-16. A fat blue spark across a 1/4 inch air gap while cranking the engine indicates the magneto is working properly. (Courtesy Champion Spark Plug Co.)

If the spark is weak, or is orange in color, or doesn't exist at all, you'll need to dig a little deeper to get things running again. The procedures described here will differ somewhat from one brand of chain saw to another, but the basics are always the same.

Do not remove any coil mounting screws. Look to see that breaker points are located behind the magneto rotor (they almost always are, but a few saws have slots that allow work to be done without removing the rotor). If the points are there, remove the starter housing to gain access to the rotor. Most modern chain saw engines will have the coil mounting screws in close proximity to the rotor, and if these are loosened, you'll have to add another operation to the tuneup. The coil core legs to rotor air gap will have to be reset with a piece of shim stock. This gap varies from make to make and can sometimes be a chore to get adjusted properly, so the work is usually done only when absolutely necessary.

Next, the rotor nut is removed. Then a puller, either the one specified by the manufacturer or a standard prong and jackscrew puller, can be used to lift out the rotor. If a puller is not available and you don't wish to buy one, hold the rotor and power head assembly off the work surface and give the end of the rotor shaft a *light* tap with a small hammer. If several such taps don't work, the puller will be needed. A hard, heavy rap with even a small hammer can damage the shaft threads, so use care. Once the rotor is removed, the crankshaft can be turned until the breaker points open (Fig. 3-17).

Now, use a dry, lintfree rag to wipe the breaker box area around the points clean. Next, examine the points for wear, pitting, or misalignment. If they are bad and must be removed, a screw releases the breaker points and the condenser. Points and condenser should be replaced at the same time. Now turn the rotor shaft until the breaker arm cam follower (made of machined fiber in most cases) rides the high spot on the crankshaft cam section just past the edge of the cam breakoff point.

Use a feeler gauge or piece of shim stock of the appropriate size to set the point gap (Fig. 3-18). Most chain saws will operate quite well at a 0.015 to 0.016 inch gap, but a few require more or less point gap and will not work without the proper gap because the point setting also sets the engine timing). Leave the gauge in place as you tighten the fixed contact screw on the points.

Fig. 3-17. A breaker point magneto unit. (Courtesy Homelite.)

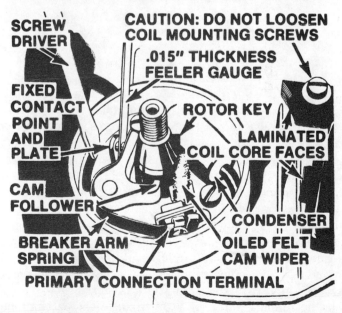

SCREW
DRIVER

CAUTION: DO NOT LOOSEN
COIL MOUNTING SCREWS

.015" THICKNESS
FEELER GAUGE

FIXED
CONTACT
POINT
AND
PLATE

ROTOR KEY

LAMINATED
COIL CORE FACES

CAM
FOLLOWER

CONDENSER

BREAKER ARM
SPRING

OILED FELT
CAM WIPER

PRIMARY CONNECTION TERMINAL

Fig. 3-18. Using a feeler gauge to set the point gap. (Courtesy Homelite.)

Remove the feeler gauge and slip a clean piece of cardboard—a business card is fine—between the points; draw it through a couple of times to clean off any grease or oil that may have gotten on the point contact surfaces. Turn the shaft to the high point of cam contact, remove the cardboard and lift the cam follower a short distance away from the cam. Let it drop back with a snap. Snapping the cam follower two or three times will clean out any small dust particles that have entered.

To reassemble, place the rotor on the shaft and then put the washer and rotor nut in place. Tighten the nut to its maximum torque setting. See the specifications chart in this chapter for other saw models. Do not overtighten the rotor shaft nut since this could damage the crankshaft; it is an expensive part to replace (Fig. 3-19).

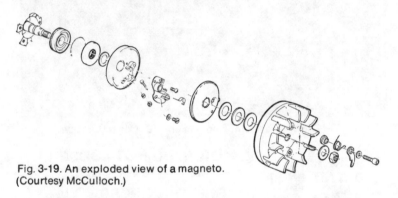

Fig. 3-19. An exploded view of a magneto. (Courtesy McCulloch.)

Timing

Homelite saws with magneto ignition have fixed timing settings. But some saws require that a timing setting be made to proper specifications. An ohmmeter makes the job of timing engines an easier one.

Here's how it's done. First, disconnect the ignition coil lead from the breaker point terminal and connect either the leads of a timing light or air ohmmeter (as the manufacturer of the meter directs). Slip a depth gauge type measuring tool in the spark plug hole and turn the engine until the piston reaches the specified distance from the top of the cylinder. At this time either the timing light should just come on or the ohmmeter should indicate "points open" by showing a break (a swing from zero ohms to infinity) in the circuit.

If the manufacturer of your timing light or ohmmeter neglected to include instructions, or included instructions as clear as a muddy river (the usual case), the setup is as follows. One lead of whichever instrument is being used is attached to ground; the other lead is attached to the movable side of the points. Nothing fancy about that, but hardly anyone ever gets it clear the first time. Check to make sure there is not a conductive oil film creating a ground from the movable side of the points. But usually if you see the points open and the light is still *on* or the ohmmeter indicates zero ohms, you can almost bet that either the points are bad or there is a short to ground somewhere in the system. If the problem does appear to be a case of "oil film ground," simply spray the points and their surrounding area with a dry-start compound.

The next step, getting the transfer to degrees on your top-dead-center setting, can create a bit of a problem. Some engines have a timing mark on the flywheel and another mark on the magneto coil to indicate the proper firing spot. If the ohmmeter indicates the points are firing when these two marks are aligned, your job is over once everything is tightened up. Always check, though, after tightening down screws and nuts on any ignition system, to make certain nothing has slipped slightly during the tightening procedure. Check the point gap and then recheck the timing. It's a lot simpler to do now than after the engine is buttoned back up all the way.

If the engine does not have a timing mark, the procedure gets more complex and difficult. The factory will normally specify the distance the piston should be from the top of the cylinder when the points are opening (Table 3-2). But this distance can be specified in one of two ways. The usual way is in degrees of crankshaft rotation; for example, 23 degrees before top dead center (BTDC). Another method expresses the distance in inches. If the distance is given in inches, it will be given in decimal fractions that must be converted to standard fractions of an inch. A ruler that does the conversions for you can be a handy tool.

If the second method is used, I recommend that the flywheel and a metal part of the engine directly across from it be pin-punched to indicate the correct timing. This way, you won't have to pull the head off each time you want to set the timing. It doesn't matter where you place these punch marks. It is just necessary to have them properly aligned and located on engine parts that are not likely to be removed.

Exhaust Port and Muffler

Exhaust port cleaning and muffler cleaning can go a long way toward returning any small two-stroke engine to its original power levels.

First, remove the muffler. You will need a soft scraping tool to clean the exhaust port (a tongue depressor or ice cream stick is fine). You must make absolutely certain the piston is covering the exhaust port while you are cleaning (Fig. 3-20). If an attempt is made to clean the port when the piston does not cover it, chunks of carbon can easily fall inside the cylinder causing extensive internal engine damage later. If such chunks do drop inside the cylinder, there is no recourse other than to remove the head, or the cylinder if it's a one-piece unit, and do a thorough cleaning job. With the piston covering the port, do as thorough a cleaning job as you can.

Fig. 3-20. Before cleaning the exhaust port, insure that the piston covers it. (Courtesy Champion Spark Plug Co.)

Chain saw mufflers are often made in two or more parts, so they are simple to clean. Separate the parts and scrape them clean. Some people will soak the parts in kerosene and light them with a match. If the parts are left to burn until they go out by themselves, much of the carbon buildup will burn off, and any that doesn't burn off will soften up and be quite easy to scrape off. Be careful if you do use this technique. Stay away from other flammables. Don't pick up the hot parts. Do not use a fluid any more volatile than kerosene for this burn-off technique, and be very careful when lighting it.

Cooling Fins

After cleaning the exhaust port and muffler, take a thin, bladelike tool to the engine cooling fins and sweep out all the accumulated chips and sawdust (Fig. 3-21). This will help prevent overheating in hard use and is a job that should be done more frequently than cleaning the exhaust port. Never fail to clean the engine cooling fins when you have the chance. Reassemble the unit and make a few cuts to check out the power levels after the saw is fully warmed up. If power has returned to, or near, original levels, you probably won't want to bother doing a full tuneup.

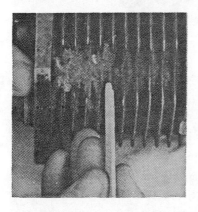

Fig. 3-21. Clean out the engine cooling fins with a bladelike tool. (Courtesy Champion Spark Plug Co.)

STARTER

Starter cord problems are among the most frequent troubles anyone will have with a chain saw. Though modern cords and recoil springs are made of high quality material, they get a lot of use. If the engine is not kept in correct tune, the starter cord and spring will get even more use.

Though the starting system looks, and is, simple, there can be a number of problems: a stretched or broken rope, weak or broken recoil springs, improper engagement of the starter at the flywheel.

Usually it's possible to figure out what has gone wrong before the unit is removed from the saw. If the spring doesn't rewind the starter rope, you can be sure that the spring is broken, has weakened badly, or has slipped its adjustment. If the yanks on the starter rope don't turn the engine over, it's a safe bet the flywheel and starter are not engaging as they should.

Fortunately, engineers who design chain saws realize the starter is a weak link and usually make the unit easy to inspect and repair. Several screws are all that hold any starter to the

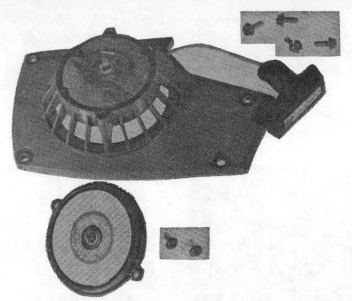

Fig. 3-22. The starter unit for a Homelite 150 Automatic.

body of the powerhead (Fig. 3-22). Remove the screws and lift the unit off, as shown in Fig. 3-23.

There may be only a need for tightening, or retensioning, the starter rope. Slippage during use and stretching of the rope

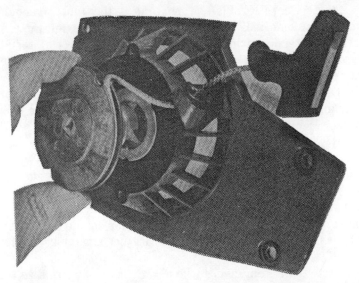

Fig. 3-23. After the screws are removed, lift off the starter unit. (Courtesy Homelite.)

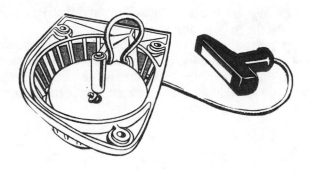

Fig. 3-24. Keep the pulley from turning as you pull the starter cord part of the way out of the starter assembly. (Courtesy Homelite.)

can account for this. Pull the rope a short way out of the starter assembly, and at the same time, keep the pulley from turning (Fig. 3-24). Wind one or more extra turns onto the pulley and pull the rope back into place so it will rewind when the pulley is released. You shouldn't have to wind the starter grip right up against the starter housing. Too much tension here can be as bad as not enough (Fig. 3-25).

When getting ready to remove the starter spring, use caution. Starter springs are quite powerful and can do severe damage if they spring loose and strike you in the face. In most chain saw starter mechanisms, you can pull the rope loose from the pulley and let the pulley unwind slowly while it is still in the starter casing. When the tension is removed, carefully tilt the pulley so that you can see where the inner spring loop

Fig. 3-25. Don't rewind all of the starter cord into the starter housing. (Courtesy Homelite.)

engages the pulley. Push the pulley toward that loop and tilt the loop until the pulley comes free of the spring.

Spring retainers are removed by pressing down on the center of the spring and using long nose pliers to pull each leg of the retainer free (Fig. 3-26). Then the rewind spring is unhooked and lifted out: again use caution, for the spring may still be under a fair amount of tension.

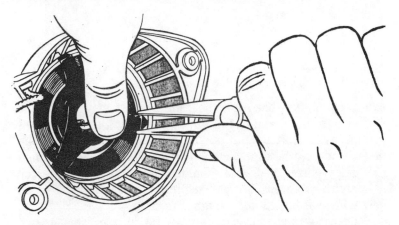

Fig. 3-26. Use long nose pliers to unseat each leg of the spring retainer. (Courtesy Homelite.)

When a new spring is to be installed, the outer ends should be checked against the old spring (Fig. 3-27). This check is essential since different chain saw makes have the outer ends pointing either right or left; installing the spring backwards fouls up the works totally. The old spring should be discarded safely in a spot where children are not likely to get their hands on it. Wrap the old spring with tape or wire to prevent its unwinding. Discarding an unwound spring is all right, except that the edges tend to be quite sharp. When installing the spring retainer on the new spring, move the legs a bit to the left or right of the original assembly position in the starter housing.

Reverse the removal procedure from this point and the new spring will go in with a minimum of difficulty.

Starter ropes are the easiest, and most frequent, repair you will encounter. The rope is threaded through the hole in the pulley (Fig. 3-28), and a double knot is tied in the end (Fig. 3-29). The rope is then pulled so the knot is tight against the hole, and excess rope is cut off. Wind the rope on the pulley

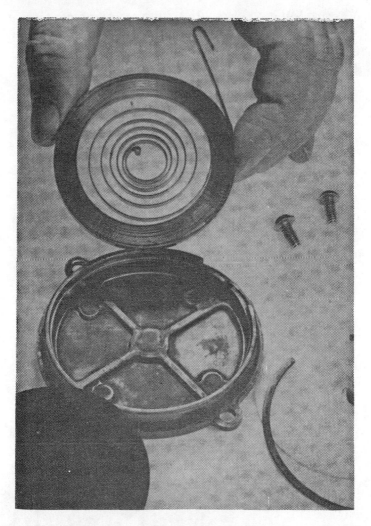

Fig. 3-27. Insure that the outer ends of a new spring are pointing in the right direction. (Courtesy Homelite.)

making sure it is wound in the same direction as was the old rope.

Line up the inner spring loop, or lugs if that's what your chain saw uses, with the retaining groove on the pulley and press the pulley into position (some saws will allow a direct press, while others will require the pulley to be tilted before pressing). Pass the rope through the hole in the starter housing; thread the rope through the grip and knot its end. Tension the starter as already described; with a new rope, most saws will need from 8 to 11 turns to get proper tension. Start with the low figure since too tight a job of tensioning will often break the spring when a hard effort is made to start the engine.

Install the starter housing so the pulley insert is matched to the flywheel.

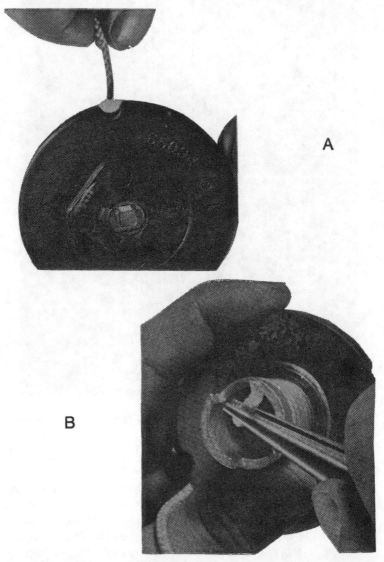

Fig. 3-28. Thread the starter cord through the hole in the pulley (A); use long nose pliers if necessary (B). (Courtesy Homelite.)

Fig. 3-29. Tie a knot in the end of the cord. (Courtesy Homelite.)

CARBURETION

Almost all chain saws today use carburetors with a diaphragm fuel pump instead of a float bowl. The diaphragm fuel pump provides the carburetor with its all-position capability because fuel is delivered at a constant rate. This feature is essential for a great many cutting jobs.

If a saw runs well, leave the carb alone. At season's end, dumping the gas tank or using a fuel stabilizer (STA-BIL is available from Knox Laboratories, Chicago, Il 60616) prevents the gooey buildup of gum and varnish deposits often formed when gasoline combines with oxygen at moderate temperatures. This step will extend the useful life of the entire fuel system.

Even with a saw that fails to start, the carburetor should usually not be touched. The problem is more likely to be located in the ignition system than it is in the fuel system. First, of course, check out the fuel. Make sure the tank is full. Check any fuel filters. Check the air filters. Then check the ignition for spark.

Carburetor adjustments normally only become necessary when spark plug readings indicate problems with the mixture. Of course, if the carburetor has been torn down for overhaul or cleaning (see the chapter on overhauls), then it must be reset. Once in a while, after breakin, a change in carburetion will be required. Such changes, though, are usually very slight, and the saw may just as easily settle into routine cutting without any adjustment.

First, locate the idle speed screw. A typical carburetor is shown in Fig. 3-30. The idle speed screw will bear on the throttle shaft or the throttle linkage and can be located by pulling the trigger and seeing which of the adjustment screws do bear on the linkage (you may have to remove the air filter cover to see the linkage on many saws). Most idle speed screws on chain saws are marked, either with a decal or a word cast in the case.

Next, locate the mixture screws (8 and 9 on Fig. 3-30). On most chain saws there will be two mixture screws, one right next to the other. If the carburetor is visible, the screws can be located by the springs on their shanks. If the screws are unmarked, the one with the thinner shank is the low-speed mixture control, while the thicker shanked screw controls the high-speed range. For minor adjustments, start the saw and let it idle for a few minutes. Make a few cuts to get the engine up to operating temperature and then let it drop back to idle.

If the idle is correct, the chain will *not* be moving on the guide bar. Turn the idle screw until the chain just starts moving. Now, keeping track of the number of turns on the screw, turn down until the engine stumbles and seems ready to stall. Moving the idle screw back half the number of turns you've counted will provide the correct idle speed. In other words, if you've turned the idle screw back three turns from the chain "creep" point to the engine stumbling point, the correct idle will be 1 1/2 turns from the point where the engine started to stumble.

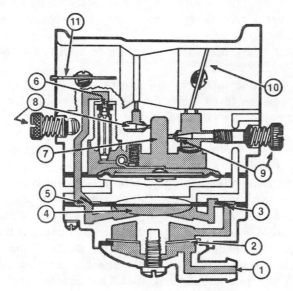

The dark areas are the fuel chambers;
light areas the air chambers.

1. Fuel inlet.

2. Fuel inlet screen (can be removed for cleaning by removing bottom screw and cover).

3. Diaphragm chamber inlet valve.

4. Fuel pump chamber. "Wet" side is underside of diaphragm..."dry" side is vented to engine. Crankcase pressure actuates diaphragm.

5. Diaphragm chamber outlet valve.

6. Needle and seat. Actuated by lever resting on diaphragm.

7. Metering chamber...next stop, main discharge jet.

8. High-speed mixture adjustment screw.

9. Idle mixture screw.

10. Throttle plate. Notice in the closed position the throttle plate rests between the idle ports.

11. Choke plate.

Fig. 3-30. Cross section of a typical chain saw carburetor. (Courtesy McCulloch.)

Turn the low speed screw until the engine gathers speed as you listen (Fig. 3-31). When the engine seems to have reached the top speed possible, check to see if the chain is moving. If it has begun to creep, you'll have to readjust the idle speed. After that, you'll have to repeat the process with the low range screw. Several repititions of each may be necessary to get things perfect.

In most cases, this adjustment will be all that's needed to tuneup a chain saw carburetor.

High speed adjustments are harder to make and require some experience to do well. Fortunately, the need for high speed adjustments should be seldom. Some saws, such as the Homelite XL-2 Automatic, do not even have a high speed adjustment. The factory adjustment is locked in and expected to last the life of the carburetor.

For high speed adjustments on those saws which provide a high speed adjustment needle (thick shanked), the procedure is as follows. First, make sure the saw is up to operating temperature. Lean the mixture (usually the mixture is leaned by turning the high speed screw clockwise so that it moves in to its seat). Open the throttle. If the saw has been leaned out enough to start the adjustment, it will not accelerate cleanly from idle to top speed; it will hesitate or stumble. Now enrich the mixture by reversing your next turn of the screw. Work in units of one-quarter to one-eighth of a turn, or even less. Continue enriching the mixture until the saw accelerates cleanly from idle to top speed without any hesitation. Further enrichment only cuts down on power and wastes fuel.

If you have a chain saw that won't start and you suspect carburetor misadjustment, the following procedures should be used.

First, turn both the high- and low-speed needles to their seats (no matter what direction you turn the screws, you'll

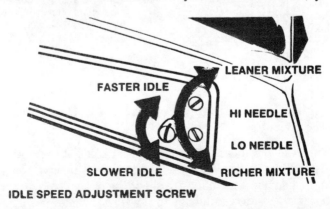

Fig. 3-31. Carburetor adjustment screws on a chain saw. (Courtesy Homelite.)

rapidly know if they're seating; if the screw comes all the way out of the carburetor, that's the wrong direction!). Do this gently. Jamming the needles into their seats will ruin them. Without good needles and smooth seats, the carburetor is useless and must be replaced. Open both needles a single turn from their seated positions. On many chain saw carburetors the correct setting is one turn plus or minus an eighth of a turn, but wear can affect this setting.

Start the saw. If the saw still won't start, continue to enrich the low speed mixture by one-eighth turn increments until it does start and will continue to run (the saw should run for at least five minutes before the rest of the carburetor adjustment process is followed).

Next, adjust the idle screw and idle mixture screw to get a correct idle, as already described, and then move through the high speed adjustment until the saw runs cleanly. Always make certain the engine is thoroughly warmed before making the final idle, low, and high speed adjustments. If the engine is cold and the choke is on, the chain may move slightly. Once the choke is off, however, the chain should stop moving completely. Never adjust any carburetor with the choke on.

Chapter 4

Chain Saw Troubleshooting

Chain Saw Troubleshooting

Chain saw troubles are often easily cured if the saw is cared for on a daily/hourly running time schedule. If proper care has been an integrated part of the chain saw's use, a simple troubleshooting checklist will usually bring the problem to light almost immediately.

Fig. 4-1 shows a performance log for chain saw use. A copy of this log should be kept near the chain saw.

Making repairs on a chain saw is not difficult. But pinpointing the troublespots can sometimes be an exasperating chore. The following troubleshooting checklist should help you find and solve the problem as quickly as possible.

Engine Cannot Be Started:

1. Check the ignition switch. Make sure it's in the *on* position.
2. Check the fuel tank. It may be dry or the fuel may be old.
3. Check the spark plug for fouling. See spark plug illustrations in the preceding chapter. Make sure the plug is gapped correctly and clean, then try to start the saw. If it still does not start, check for spark strength. If there is spark, go to number 4 in this list. If there is no spark, test the ignition switch with an

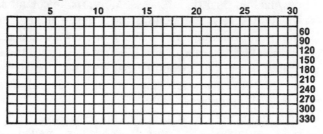

Fig. 4-1. Chain saw performance log. (Courtesy Homelite.)

ohmmeter to make sure there is continuity when the switch is *on*.

4. Fuel may not be reaching the carburetor. First, to make sure, remove the air filter and check the barrel of the carburetor. The barrel's walls should be damp with gas. If the walls are not moist, check to see that the choke is actually closing. If it is, and the barrel remains dry, check for a plugged fuel filter. If the filter is all right, you can move on to carburetor fuel and pulse lines (the pulse line feeds crankcase vacuum pulsations to the carburetor to help regulate fuel feed). Check these lines for splitting, cracking, and kinking. Replace or straighten as needed.

5. The starting speed may be adjusted too low. Adjust the throttle latch mechanism, if the saw has one, to increase the speed setting with the throttle locked open. If this causes the engine to start, you will have to

87

readjust the carburetor for correct starting speed and recheck the throttle latch assembly afterwards. If the saw has no throttle latch assembly, make certain that the idle screw is touching the throttle linkage, and move on to the idle mixture screw (low speed screw). Richen the idle mixture in 1/8 turn steps until the saw starts, and go through the complete carburetor adjustment series described in Chapter 3 until the saw runs well and starts easily.

6. Low compression. If there is no resistance from the engine when the starter cord is pulled, low compression may be the cause. Low compression itself is caused by several things. If your chain saw has a large engine, there may be a compression release valve. This valve may stick open and not allow the fuel mix to be compressed properly prior to ignition. Check the valve if there is one. If the compression release valve is functioning properly, or there is no compression release valve on the saw, refer to the chapter on engine overhauls. Problems could start with simple engine wear, too much piston wear, cylinder wall wear, or a blown piston. Usually the engine will have to be dismantled to find the cause. Low compression for any of the engine internal causes listed will usually require an engine overhaul.

Engine starts, produces full power then dies:

1. Check the valve or filter in the fuel cap. You can determine if this filter is clogged by opening the cap about a fifth of a turn and then starting the chain saw. If the saw runs well until you tighten the cap, clean or replace the check valve or filter.

Engine runs fine then misses or stalls out:

1. This problem will be caused by ignition wire shorts against the frame of the saw. Check the ingition leads for bare spots or badly worn spots (high voltage can jump through insulation if it is not thick enough). Tape any shorting leads with plastic electrician's tape, or use a silicone sealant to insulate the short. Silicone

sealant, allowed to dry and then covered with plastic tape, is the best solution, particularly if the short has been caused by abrasion.

Engine starts but dies under a load:

1. Check the fuel system for air leaks. Make the first check along the fuel lines, and then check the base of the carburetor for air leaks. Use a soap and water solution to see if there is any bubbling around the base of the carburetor and along the fuel lines. Kerosene can also be used to trace the leaks, but it's harder to see the bubbles, although there is less chance of contaminating the fuel. Thick oil applied to the base of the carburetor will also supply an answer. If the saw works fine with a deposit of oil around the carb base, then there's a leak and the oil is sealing it temporarily.
2. Too lean a high speed mixture can cause the engine to stall under a load. Adjust for a richer mixture as shown in the carburetor section in Chapter 3.
3. A faulty pulse line can cause stallout under a load. Check for kinks, cracks, or splits. Replace the line as necessary.
4. Faulty fuel pumps or carburetors can also be the cause. Refer to the overhaul section for carburetor pressure testing and repair information.

Engine lacks speed and power and smokes a lot:

1. Too rich a mixture will cause a drop in top speed and overall power output. Refer to the section on carburetor adjustments in Chapter 3. Adjust the carburetor for the best combination of speed and power.
2. If the carburetor inlet needle is set too high, the same problem occurs. If the carburetor will not come into adjustment during the detailed adjusting procedure, the inlet needle is probably the difficulty. Refer to the major overhaul chapter for information on working with carburetor internals.
3. Too much oil in the fuel mixture may cause the problem. Spark plug reading and using the photos in Chapter 3 will tell if this is happening. Use the correct fuel mixture.

Engine lacks power but does not smoke:

1. If the engine has a compression release valve, it is either leaking or stuck open. Thoroughly clean the area to free a stuck valve and replace one that is leaking.

Engine won't idle smoothly:

1. The carburetor idle adjustment may be incorrectly set. If the idle speed is correct, then the mixture must be incorrect. Possibly the idle stop screw has been set high (for more speed) because the low-speed mixture needle has been adjusted too lean. Adjust to correct running as detailed in the carburetor section of Chapter 3. The idle speed may be adjusted too low. Readjust the idle speed, check the running of the saw, and readjust the mixture control if necessary. Refer to the section on carburetor adjustment.

2. The low-speed mixture needle or its seat may be damaged. If the needle is bent or damaged in any way, replace it. If the seat appears to be damaged, the carburetor will have to be replaced. Refer to the section on carburetor overhaul in the overhaul Chapter.

3. Dirt in the carburetor idle system will cause a rough idle. Clean the carburetor as covered in the section on carburetor overhaul.

4. The fuel system or the carburetor may be leaking air. Check for obvious leaks with a soap and water solution, or as covered in *Engine starts but dies under a load*. Replace any leaking parts such as gaskets and fuel lines.

5. An air leak through a cracked carburetor connector or through engine walls or seals may also cause a rough idle. Disassemble, check, and reinstall the carburetor (see overhaul chapter for details). If that doesn't cure the problem, the engine should be pressure tested at the dealer's shop (this procedure is nearly impossible for the home mechanic).

6. A faulty clutch assembly may also cause a rough idle. Check below in this chapter for clutch slipping and grabbing solutions.

7. Ignition misfires at low speed can also cause a rough idle. Ignition misfire can be checked by taping a neon

test lamp to the high voltage coil when the engine is idling. If the lamp indicates erratic firing, continue with ignition checks as covered in the major overhaul section.

Engine runs too hot:

This can be a major problem with two-stroke engines, so a careful watch must be kept. An engine running too hot for too long will soon break down.

1. Check the fuel mixture ingredients. Use only the correct two-stroke oil and fresh gasoline, mixed in the proportions recommended by the manufacturer of the oil.
2. Check the spark plug for type and heat range. Refer to Table 3-2 or call your dealer for any saws not listed.
3. Dirty air intake screens in the air cooling system can cause overheating. Check and clean the screens around the starter housing and install a clean air filter (clean the one on the saw, when possible). Remove the starter housing and poke and blow all debris out of the engine cooling fins. If necessary, disassemble the rear powerhead housing and clean all the cooling fins.
4. Too lean carburetor operation can cause overheating. Refer to *Engine starts but dies under a load* in this section and check out and eliminate all air leaks or fuel blockages.
5. If all else fails, readjust the carburetor to a richer setting.

Engine floods with fuel:

1. Dirt under the carburetor inlet needle, or an inlet needle set too high are the usual causes of engine flooding, but sometimes the inlet lever spring will slip off its dimpled detent and flood the saw. Check the overhaul chapter for carburetor disassembly and cleaning information or have your dealer make the repairs.

Engine misfires:

1. If the choke remains closed or partially closed as the engine warms up, the resulting overrich mixture can

cause misfiring. Operate only with the choke in a fully opened position after initial warmup. Check the choke to make sure it's opening fully. The fault will usually be with the operator; mechanical choke linkages used in chain saw engines seldom malfunction. If the choke does malfunction, check the overhaul chapter for information on carburetor disassembly.

Engine runs after the ignition is shut off:

1. A faulty ignition switch or ignition switch lead is the usual cause of this problem in a relatively new chain saw. Check both the switch and the lead by connecting either an ohmmeter or a test light from the ground screw lead of the ignition module to the terminal of the switch. The meter should indicate no continuity when the switch is in its *on* or *run* position but should indicate continuity when the switch is thrown to *stop* or *off*. Repair or replace the switch or the lead as indicated. The overhaul chapter covers ignition work and switch assembly construction.

2. Dieseling is another name for the "run-on" effect. If is caused by spark plug fouling or by carbon fouling on parts of the cylinder or piston (burrs on port edges can become heated to the point where they fire the mixture after the engine is shut down). Such dieseling can cause major engine damage in short order. If the ignition switch and lead check out all right, remove and check the spark plug. Use the photographs in Chapter 3 and look for carbon or oil fouling. If the plug is only lightly fouled, clean it, regap it, and reinstall it after checking the spark plug hole to try to locate any deposits or flashing which could heat during the engine's cycling and cause dieseling. Remove any such deposits, either through the spark plug hole or through the exhaust port after the muffler is removed. Now replace the clean and correctly gapped spark plug and test the saw. When removing carbon, use only a soft scraper, such as an ice cream stick, and make sure that any carbon scraped free is shaken out of the spark plug hole or the exhaust port. If the saw continues to diesel, you'll have to remove the head or cylinder to check the cylinder walls, cylinder head and

ports, and the piston crown for deposits or flashed metal left over from casting. Scrape off any deposits, remove any flashing, and reassemble. See the overhaul chapter for details of disassembly and assembly.

Chain receiving too little oil:

1. Check the chain oil reservoir for fluid. Fill, if needed, and recheck the lubrication.
2. Some saws have small knobs to adjust the flow of chain oil, but these are usually found only on professional chain saws or top-of-the-line homeowner's models. Turn the knob in the correct direction to increase the oil flow, and check the flow.
3. The most common fault, after a dry reservoir, is sawdust or small chops clogging the oil discharge hole in the chain saw guide bar or guide bar mounting plate. If this is the case, remove the guide bar and use a stiff piece of wire to clean the oil hole in the bar and the hole in the mounting pad. Pay special attention to the oil discharge hole in the mounting pad to be sure that all dust or chips removed come out. They must not get forced back into the oil lines. Continue circling the guide bar to remove all sawdust in the chain tang groove. If not removed, this debris will be forced into the oil discharge holes. Check the chain's drive tangs for sharpness. If the drive tangs are not sharp, they will not clean the guide bar groove properly. Sharpen every third or fourth drive tang with an oval file of the correct size; see the chapter on chains and guide bars for details.
4. Chain oil pump seals leaking. Remove the "O" ring and replace it. Refer to the section on oil pumps in the overhaul chapter.
5. Oil line pickup screen clogged. Check and clean if needed. Refer to the overhaul chapter for details.
6. Oil line leaking air into the system. Inspect and replace if needed. Refer to the overhaul chapter.

Clutch slips or grabs:

1. Cutting at less than full throttle will wear or glaze the clutch surfaces. Always make your cuts at full

throttle. Replace or repair clutch as required. See the overhaul chapter's section on clutches.

2. A worn, dirty, or scored clutch will cause grabbing, as will a clutch that has become bent or cracked. Replace or repair as needed. Refer to overhaul chapter, clutch section.

3. Chain and bar difficulties, including incorrect chain tension, burred guide-bar rails, and poor general chain maintenance can cause grabbing or slipping of the clutch. Read and follow all instructions in the section on chain adjustment and the chain care chapter.

Chain chatters or bucks, or grabs and cuts roughly:

1. Chain tension too loose. Readjust according to directions in Chapter 3.

2. The depth gauges are set too low or the area is not shaped properly. Contour the depth gauges correctly and sharpen the teeth of the chain to raise the gauges to their proper height. Refer to the chapter on chain care for details.

3. A worn drive sprocket will cause irregular chain movement, resulting in some or all of the above problems. If the drive sprocket teeth come to a very sharp point or are hooked, replace the sprocket. When the sprocket is replaced, the chain should also be replaced. If you are using a sprocket nose guide bar, that sprocket should be replaced at the same time the drive sprocket is replaced. Refer to the overhaul chapter for details on drive sprocket replacement, and to the chain care chapter for nose sprocket replacement and chain filing details.

4. Incorrect filing angles when sharpening the chain can cause problems, particularly if a side plate becomes hooked while filing is being done. Refile the chain. Refer to the chapter on chain care for details on corrective filing.

Chain will not cut rapidly:

1. Check the chain for dullness (a dull chain cutting edge will reflect light, but a sharp edge will not). Sharpen. Refer to sharpening details in the chapter on chain care.

2. Wrong filing angles can reduce chain cutting efficiency. Refile to the correct angles. Refer to corrective filing details in the chain care chapter.

3. Depth gauges set too high will cause a drop in cutting speed. Lower the gauges to their correct depth after every third sharpening. Or have your dealer do the job every third sharpening; just make sure he sets the depth gauges each time he sharpens the chain. Sharpening is easier than setting depth gauges, so for most people it's worthwhile to have the dealer sharpen the chain every third time just to get the gauges set correctly. Refer to the chapter on chain care if you wish to set your own depth gauges.

4. Chain tension set too tight will also reduce cutting efficiency and speed. Adjust your chain tension to the standard for the type of guide bar being used. See the chapter on chains for details.

5. Pinched, spread, or burred guide-bar rails can cause a binding of the chain as it passes the malformed spot. Repair spread rails by gently tapping them together with a hammer. If possible, a soft-faced hammer should be used. Repair pinched rails by gently prying them apart with a screwdriver. File off any burrs. The key to working on the guide bar is gentleness. The hardened steel used for the bar doesn't ruin easily, but if it does get damaged, the cost of replacement is among the highest for parts outside the engine.

6. Abrasion damage to the chain's cutting teeth will certainly reduce cutting efficiency. If teeth are broken completely off, replace the entire chain. However, if teeth are partially broken, you can file them to correct the damage. File away the damaged area, including any teeth which have become dechromed. Since all teeth must be filed to the same size, undamaged teeth must also be filed down. Refer to the chapter on chain care.

7. Guide-bar grooves wear as the chain saw gets a lot of use. If chain tension has been incorrect, the wear may be mostly along one side of the bar groove, which can force the chain to ride one side rail. The result can stall the chain in the cut. Replace the guide bar and maintain proper chain tension on the new guide bar.

Reversing the guide bar every five hours or so will help equalize wear on the tip.

Chain dulls immediately after being sharpened:
1. Cutters, or teeth, filed to a feather edge will loose that edge almost immediately. Refile to the correct edge pattern. Refer to the chapter on chain care.
2. Too much top-plate angle or side-plate hook will also cause immedaite chain dulling. Refile to the proper angle to correct the condition. Again, refer to the chapter on chain care for details.
3. A chain can dull quickly if it is adjusted too tightly, used with too little chain oil, or pinched in the guide bar. Replace the chain or, if it hasn't been ruined, refile. Check the oil pump output (refer to the chapter on overhaul) after checking that there is oil in the reservoir. Maintain proper chain tension at all times. Spread the guide bar rails so that the chain drive tangs are not pinched.

Chain gets too loose on the guide bar:
1. If the chain is new, it may require adjusting as frequently as every half hour for a period of several hours. All new chains stretch and take time to break in. Keep the tension as close to correct as possible until the stretching stops.
2. Too much pressure brought to bear on the saw in a cut will cause chain stretch. If you sharpen the chain correctly, the excess pressure will not be needed to make the cuts.
3. Burred bar rails can cause drag and stretch the chain. Smooth the guide bar rails with a file.
4. If the chain doesn't receive enough oil for heavy duty cutting, it will heat and stretch. Make sure the oil discharge holes in the guide bar mounting pad and the guide bar itself are clear of sawdust and dirt. Where possible, adjust the oiler for a greater oil delivery. If the saw has both an automatic and manual oiler, use the manual oiler to supplement the automatic oiler. When there is no way to adjust the amount of oil being delivered, and when the guide-bar mounting pad and guide-bar oil holes are clean, and when there is no

supplementary manual oiler, use a spray can to add oil to the bar and chain during heavy cutting.

5. If the chain is loose on the bar initially, it will loosen even more as it heats from normal cutting friction. Let the chain cool a bit, then adjust it for warm chain conditions. Refer to the chapter on chain care.

6. When a chain is too bluntly filed or is just plain dull, it will heat up and get loose quickly. Refer to the chapter on chain care.

Chain rides high in bar groove:

1. A sawdust-packed bar groove will force the chain to ride well up in the groove. Clean the groove with a short length of stiff wire and refile at least every fourth link of the chain's drive tangs so that the sharp edges will clear sawdust from the groove. Refer to the chapter on chain care.

2. Bar groove rails wear down eventually. The chain will then ride too high. The bar can be regrooved at least once by a dealer with a well equipped machine shop, or the bar can be replaced. Refer to the chapter on chain care for details on bar and chain installation.

Saw does not cut straight:

1. When the teeth on one side of a chain become damaged, the saw will tend to twist in the cut, making cutting in a straight line nearly impossible. Sharpen damaged cutters, making sure to remove the entire damaged area. Next, sharpen the cutters on the other side of the chain to the same length. Refer to the chapter on chain care for details on corrective filing.

2. Unequal filing angles or unequal cutter lengths can have a drastic effect on the quality of a cut. File all cutters to the same angles and lengths. This is more easily done if a device such as the File 'n' Joint is used.

3. If some depth gauges are higher than others or have become different in their finished contours, the saw will also pull in the cut. Lower all depth gauges to the same height and shape them for smooth feeding of the chain through the cut. This job can be done by a dealer if you're not using a File 'n' Joint or File 'n' Guide

device or if you don't have a depth gauge. Refer to the chapter on chain care.

The first step with any sort of engine troubleshooting is to learn what a healthy engine sounds like and get the feel of how it runs. The first few times a chain saw is run, the operator should pay close attention to the sound, feel, and cutting speed of the saw. Once you become familiar with normal saw operation, you'll be much quicker to recognize troubles with the saw if they do occur. You'll probably catch troubles long before they reach a serious stage, thus saving yourself time and money.

Still, the best rule to follow when working with any small engine is the one of beneficient neglect. Do the recommended maintenance at the appropriate intervals, but don't fool with adjustments until the need for making changes becomes absolutely clear.

If you've taken the time and trouble to become familiar with the operation of your chain saw, you'll know just when changes are needed, and a quick look at this chapter will speedily show you how to correct almost any problem the saw is likely to have.

You'll notice that at least half the problems one can expect from a chain saw involve the chain. Correct sharpening of a chain can take one half hour or so using only a file and file holder. With a few specialized tools such as the File 'n' Joint described in the chapter on chain care, the job can be shortened considerably. There are also inexpensive electric sharpening devices which will shorten the job to not much more than 5 minutes and eliminate 99 percent of the work involved. But you still may prefer to spend a few dollars to have a dealer sharpen your chain, especially if you don't use the saw a great deal. If that's the case, keep at least one extra chain on hand at all times for there may be times when the dealer can't do the job in time.

Chapter 5
Major Chain
Saw Servicing

Major Chain Saw Servicing

Most of us would certainly prefer to leave major engine servicing to a capable mechanic. But in today's world that's seldom possible, for there is a real shortage of capable mechanics—well-trained people who care about the work they're doing and charge reasonable prices. Most small engine mechanics charge a good deal less than most automotive mechanics, but they still must make a living in a world where costs have risen rapidly. For that reason, even $8 an hour mechanics are hard to find today. Most want a good deal more, and if the mechanic works in a dealer's shop, the hourly cost will be marked up to cover profit, rent, tools, and overhead, including such stiff charges as heat and utilities.

We all end up thinking the cost roller coaster has no down side. Yet everyone claims to be losing money or having a hard time just getting by. That's why the old tool kit comes out more and more. A book of specifications is broken open. The screws start to come out of the engine cowlings. With luck, a few good directions, and plenty of patience, the home mechanic can make most of the repairs a good shop mechanic can. There are a few jobs the average home mechanic will not tackle. In almost all such cases, however, it's a matter of not buying tools that may be used no more than once a lifetime. There's really little point in buying pressure-testing machinery, for example, when you can take a small engine or carburetor to a dealer and have him do the pressure testing for about half the cost of the equipment. Some gear pullers and flywheel pullers can run into moderate expense but may get used about twice in a person's lifetime. Torque wrenches marked in inch- and foot-pounds rapidly become essential to a proper job if the head or cylinder comes off. In fact, the careful mechanic is even going to look up torque readings for the spark plug and use a torque wrench every time the plug is replaced or removed for maintenance. Torque wrenches rapidly add to the cost of a toolbox; even the cheapest beam style units cost over $15. The more accurate micrometer click-stop styles cost upwards of $40. It all comes down to your desires and needs. One hundred bucks invested in tools will allow you to do almost any job short of pressure testing the crankcase and carburetor on a two-stroke engine. If the tools will be useful for other jobs, then all is well and good. It's a choice each person must make, and the possibility of using tools for other work makes the choice for spending the hundred bucks much more reasonable. If the tools are only to serve that one purpose, the odds are excellent that you'll be better off letting the dealer handle your service and repair headaches. After all, a hundred bucks will buy a lot of service on a small engine.

CARBURETOR SERVICING

Since the carburetor is one of the parts most likely to wear out while the original owner has the chain saw, we can start right there.

First though, a preliminary note is in order. To prevent repairs, care of the air filtration system is essential. First and foremost is the injunction against running any engine without an air filter, even during short-term bursts while tuning and testing the saw. The air filter will, in some manner, be connected with the carburetor air horn. It can be directly mounted to the air horn, or it can be mounted to a still air box connected to the horn. The filter is usually made of either felt, paper, or plastic foam. Plastic foam types are the least often used, but are generally the best if you can locate one for your model saw. These are usually soaked in oil after being washed in gasoline and wrung out. If you use an oiled foam type filter as either a replacement or as original equipment, make certain the oil used to soak the filter is the same as that used in the fuel mixture for the engine. Some two-stroke oils are incompatible with each other and may cause gumming and plug fouling if combined. Though the chance of such a problem becoming severe enough to cause engine damage is remote, it's still best to choose an engine oil for your two-stroke saw engine at the start of its lifetime and stay with that oil until the saw is retired.

Paper and felt elements for air filters vary in their cleaning methods. All paper and some felt elements are cleaned by tapping gently against a clean, hard surface. Often a vacuum cleaner can be used on both types to get heavier dust off. Many felt filters can be washed in detergent and water, rinsed, dried, and reinstalled on the carburetor. It's smartest, in the case of washable filters, to have an extra filter or two on hand so the original can thoroughly dry before being returned to the saw.

At the end of each cutting season, or at any time when the saw will be laid up for more than a couple of weeks, the gas tank should be emptied or filled with Sta-Bil to keep gum and varnish deposits from forming. At the start of each cutting season, fill the tank with a fresh fuel mixture and give it a visual check for leaks.

When the filtration, gas tank, and lines are checked and cared for, the final fuel system element to be considered is the carburetor. On almost all chain saws, a diaphragm style carburetor is used. One or two manufacturers produce their own carburetors, but many carburetors come from Tillotson and Walbro. McCulloch is the largest chain saw manufacturer using its own carburetor, but even they use some Walbro SDC and Tillotson models. Pioneer uses its own diaphragm carburetor on some saws—Tillotson HU diaphragm carburetors on others. Their model P40 uses a Tillotson HS. For this reason, we will confine this section to Walbro and Tillotson carburetors. Even foreign saws such as the Solo and Stihl use Tillotson carburetors, so such coverage will allow you to repair and adjust probably 90 percent of today's chain saws market.

Carburetors are marked by brand and type; use those designations to order the correct rebuild kits. Make sure, though, that you take the right letters from the carburetor; Tillotson makes chain saw carburetors with the following designations: HC, HJ, HL, HU, and HS. A one letter miss will buy you the wrong parts packet. In general, the Walbro carburetors used on chain saws will be one of the HDC or SDC models, but the letters will often be followed by a number designating the specific model. Make sure you get the right prefix letters and suffix numbers.

Actually, just a simple understanding of carburetor theory is all that's really needed to rebuild a chain saw carburetor. Usually the job is a simple matter of replacing parts the manufacturer supplies in a rebuild kit. A carburetor rebuild does require manual dexterity and patience because the majority of the parts are quite small. Use a clean surface with good, steady support for your work area. As you disassemble the carburetor, lay the parts out in the order in which they were removed from the unit. This won't provide a perfect outline of how things go back together, but it will give an indication of where you are and how far you still have to go as the work progresses. Such a technique also helps to prevent leftover parts at the end of the job!

Walbro HDC

For illustration, we'll cover two of the major carburetors in use today, the Walbro HDC and the Tillotson HU. The Walbro HDC carburetor (Fig. 5-1) has a relatively small number of parts, which means procedures for service and rebuild are simpler than might be expected.

How It Works. In operation, four circuits (inlet, main, idle throttle, and clearing) are in use. Incoming fuel always passes through the main adjustment needle and the main circuit; it travels at least as far as the screen covering the disc-shaped check valve in the main jet. Whether the fuel is blocked by the check valve or flows through the main jet depends on the throttle position. During idle, the flow is blocked by the check valve, so it flows past the screen into the idle circuit where it is metered by the low-speed needle. When the throttle is opened, the clearing circuit clears the idle circuit of fuel by blowing the mixture through the main jet. During full throttle operation, the clearing circuit uses engine pulse pressure (crankcase pressure) to keep the idle circuit clear of fuel. This feature prevents engine flooding during deceleration.

Engine pulsations transmitted through the pulse tube operate the fuel pump which moves fuel from tank to carburetor inlet needle valve. This inlet needle is opened by

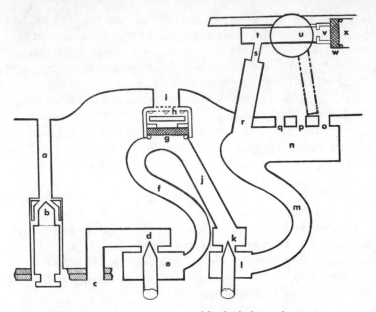

a. inlet passage from pump
b. inlet needle
c. fuel take-off
d. main needle seat
e. main needle well
f. main channel
g. main jet screen
h. main check valve
i. main jet
j. channel f to k
k. idle needle seat
l. idle needle well
m. idle fuel channel
n. idle port
o. idle (discharge) port hole
p. idle (air bleed) port hole
q. idle (air bleed) port hole
r. cross-drilled clearing channel
s. restriction in r.
t. clearing channel
u. throttle shaft valve (open)
v. limiting jet
w. screen
x. engine pulse hole

Fig. 5-1. A Walbro HDC carburetor. (Courtesy Homelite.)

the inlet lever which is actuated by movement of the metering diaphragm. The diaphragm responds to vacuum transmitted through the main jet or the idle port when the engine is running. An inlet lever spring keeps the needle seated at all other times.

When the disc-shaped check valve in the main jet is moved off its seat, it actuates the main diaphragm which then opens the fuel inlet valve. Fuel flows past the metering point of the high speed adjustment needle to a compartment where it is channeled through a curved circuit to the screen covering the main, or high speed, jet. While the throttle is open, no fuel moves through the idle port holes because engine pulse pressure is positive and back flushes the idle circuit.

Closing the throttle moves the valving hole in the shaft out of line with the limiting jet to block pulse vibrations to the idle circuit and close down the rush of air through the carburetor venturi area. Thus the high speed jet is cut out of the system. The fuel now moves across the main jet screen, through a hole, and on to the low speed needle in the curved idle circuit. With an empty idle circuit, this delayed patch prevents the carburetor from loading up when the saw decelerates quickly.

Accelerating the engine opens the main jet valve to start fuel discharge through the main jet. The throttle shaft valve also opens to restore positive pulse pressure and cut the idle circuit out of the system. The extra fuel flushed from the idle circuit keeps the saw from faltering during acceleration.

Disassembly. To ready the carburetor for disassembly, remove it from the engine and place the unit on a clean work surface. Before starting work, all gas should be drained out, in a well ventilated area.

Refer to Fig. 5-2. Unscrew the large cover screw and lift off the fuel pump cover. Next remove the fuel pump gasket and the diaphragm. On the offset end of the carburetor find four screws with external tooth lock washers. Remove these. The metering diaphragm can now be lifted off. This removal will bring into view a circuit plate with a positioning tab visible on it. This plate holds down the inlet needle, lever, and spring assembly. Remove the two flat head circuit plate screws and lift off the plate. Remove the inlet needle, lever, and spring. The removal of the thick, black circuit gasket will expose all of the fuel passages and idle ports. The high and low fuel needles and their spring assemblies can now also be removed.

During normal disassembly, you'll never need to remove the screen retaining rings and the screens covering the limiting jet or the main jet check valve.

Should you need to replace the throttle shaft, remove its screw and the throttle valve, or butterfly. Next, take out the screw and the throttle stop. The throttle shaft and lever assembly can then be gently pulled out of the carburetor body. Be extremely careful not to allow the throttle return spring to fly out. Even such small springs can do a fair amount of traveling and are then very hard to locate for reassembly.

If the choke friction spring and ball, or the choke shaft, or the valve plate itself need replacement, remove the choke valve from its shaft. Using one finger, cover the hole through

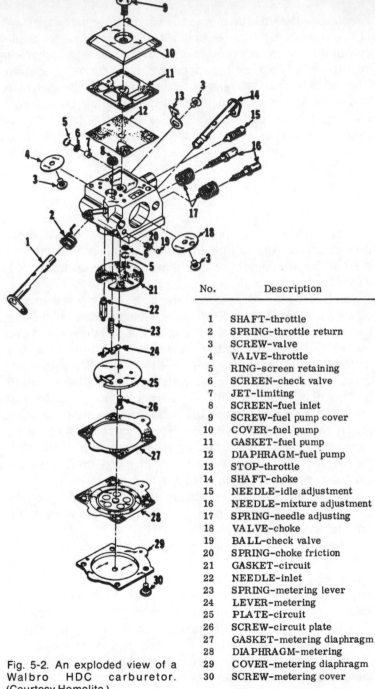

No.	Description
1	SHAFT-throttle
2	SPRING-throttle return
3	SCREW-valve
4	VALVE-throttle
5	RING-screen retaining
6	SCREEN-check valve
7	JET-limiting
8	SCREEN-fuel inlet
9	SCREW-fuel pump cover
10	COVER-fuel pump
11	GASKET-fuel pump
12	DIAPHRAGM-fuel pump
13	STOP-throttle
14	SHAFT-choke
15	NEEDLE-idle adjustment
16	NEEDLE-mixture adjustment
17	SPRING-needle adjusting
18	VALVE-choke
19	BALL-check valve
20	SPRING-choke friction
21	GASKET-circuit
22	NEEDLE-inlet
23	SPRING-metering lever
24	LEVER-metering
25	PLATE-circuit
26	SCREW-circuit plate
27	GASKET-metering diaphragm
28	DIAPHRAGM-metering
29	COVER-metering diaphragm
30	SCREW-metering cover

Fig. 5-2. An exploded view of a Walbro HDC carburetor. (Courtesy Homelite.)

which the choke shaft can be seen and pull the shaft out. Next, tilt the carburetor to remove the ball and spring from the hole.

Cleaning and Inspection. To clean and inspect the carburetor, a solvent will be needed. Homelite's service department recommends a standard solvent and not a carburetor cleaner type solution. The standard solvent is gentler and is just as effective if a carburetor is allowed to remain in its bath long enough. Soak the body and all metal parts until gum and varnish deposits disappear. Gentle brushing with a soft bristled brush may help on the carburetor body.

Any cracked, torn, or frayed internal gaskets must be replaced. Actually, it's best to replace all carburetor gaskets when doing such a complete disassembly, especially if the carburetor has seen long service. When the gaskets are replaced, the diaphragms should also be replaced.

When inspecting the carburetor, check carefully for wear around the main jet check valve, the inlet needle seat, and the limiting jet. If any of these areas do show signs of wear or damage from scratching, the carburetor cannot be rebuilt. A new body will be needed.

When checking the inlet needle, lever, and spring, look especially hard at the needle top and at the lever contact area. Any wear in either of these areas indicates a need for new parts. Make absolutely certain the limiting jet is clean and open by blowing through the jet with the throttle in the open position.

Next, examine the three fine-mesh screens. These must be open and perfectly clean. The choke friction ball must also be perfectly round. If there is any trouble at all with the screens, they should be replaced. If there is any sign of wear, no matter how slight, the choke friction ball should also be replaced.

Check the diaphragm lever. If the lever is set too high, the carburetor will flood. The lever must be set *flush* with the bottom flange of the carburetor.

Examine the inlet needle valve. If any dirt settles under the inlet needle valve, the needle cannot seat properly. Remove the needle and clean it and its seat thoroughly.

Check the circuit gasket. A leaking circuit gasket will cause flooding. If it is damaged or worn, replace.

Check the metering lever spring. If the metering lever spring doesn't seat in the dimple on the metering lever, it is improperly assembled. Take down and reassemble so that the spring seats in the dimple.

Check the fuel pump diaphragm. A leak in this diaphragm will cause flooding. Examine for cracks and pinholes by shining a flashlight on the opposite side. Sometimes diaphragm material can become porous. Should the carburetor continue to flood after all the above checks have been made, replace the fuel pump diaphragm even though it might appear to be perfect.

Examine the second and third idle holes. Dirt in either or both of these two holes will cause flooding. Check and clean if necessary.

Check the metering lever. If this lever is set too low, the fuel/air mixture ratios will constantly be too lean. Set the lever *flush* with the bottom flange of the carburetor.

Check the idle channel. Dirt in the idle channels will prevent proper adjustment and force too lean a mixture. Remove the circuit gasket and clean the channels completely.

Examine the metering diaphragm. A leak in this diaphragm will cause too lean a condition. Check as you would the fuel pump diaphragm and replace if needed. Again, a porous condition of the diaphragm material might not show up during a check. If all other checks are made and the carburetor still operates too lean, replace the metering diaphragm.

Check the crankcase to carburetor pulse line. If this line is clogged or kinked, lean running will occur. Remove any obstructions of kinks. Replace the line if necessary.

Check the manifold gaskets. Main carburetor mounting gaskets with leaks will cause a lean running condition. Examine and replace the gaskets if necessary.

Examine the fuel pump diaphragm check valve. Wear in this area will cause a lean running condition. Replace the fuel pump diaphragm.

Though a chain saw that runs too rich can drive an operator wild, the biggest problems occur when the engine runs too lean. Take special care to prevent lean engine operation.

After disassembly, cleaning, and service procedures are followed, it's time to put that mass of parts back together again.

On the Walbro HDC, the manufacturer calls for a torque reading on outside screws 6 1/2 inch-pounds, with the exception of the pump cover screw.

Assembly. Lay out all parts in the order in which they were removed. The exploded drawing provided with your rebuild kit will be a great aid here, as will Fig. 5-2.

To begin, drop the friction spring and ball into the hole crossing the choke shaft bore. Next, push the choke shaft into place in the bore. Move the choke lever to make certain the friction device is holding the choke in its open and closed positions. The edges of the choke valve are beveled to fit the carburetor barrel, and the choke valve is installed on the choke shaft with a single valve screw. Make certain the valve closes off the barrel perfectly, but also be positive there is no sticking or binding when the lever is worked. Either problem will defeat the carburetor rebuild.

If the throttle return spring has been removed, slide it back onto the throttle shaft. The hooked end of the spring will engage the notch in the shaft lever, while the straight end of the spring must be engaged in the slot in the body of the carburetor when the shaft is pushed into that body. The stop will then come in contact with the adjustment screw. The throttle valve also has beveled edges to fit the carburetor barrel as tightly as possible without binding. Assemble the throttle valve to the shaft with the remaining valve screw and check for bind. If there is no binding, the fit should be perfect.

Turn the carburetor over and drop the inlet needle valve into its valve seat. Position the inlet metering lever spring in the spring recess of the chamber. Now fit the circuit gasket in its proper position in the carburetor fuel chamber.

Next, position the spring on the dimple of the lever and slide the lever fork onto the needle while installing the circuit plate. Hold down the plate and make a check of the action of the needle, lever, and spring assembly. If the action is correct, there will be no binding, so fasten the circuit plate in place with the two flathead screws. Check to make sure the spring has not slipped off its dimple; should that happen, the carburetor would flood during operation.

Next, the metering diaphragm gasket, diaphragm, and cover, should be assembled, in that order. Fit them onto the carburetor with the four external-tooth lock washers and screws. Next, the fuel pump gasket, pump diaphragm, and pump cover are to be added, in that order, to the assembly on the carburetor body. The large cover screw is used to hold them in place.

Pressure testing is the final step that should be carried out when reassembling a carburetor. As mentioned earlier, pressure-testing equipment is something most home mechanics won't want to bother with. Though the expense is not overwhelming, it is something that will probably not be used very often. Usually a dealer with a decently equipped shop will be glad to do this work for a small charge.

For those who do have a pressure-testing kit and a source of air pressure of 10 pounds per square inch, the procedure is as follows. Connect the tester to the fuel pump outlet. If the tester is of the bulb type, squeeze the bulb until the reading reaches 5 pounds per square inch. If the gauge holds the pressure, the fuel pump, inlet seat, inlet needle, and metering diaphragm are in good shape and not leaking. A rebuilt carburetor can be expected to leak at least a little bit until it has undergone a half hour of use; a new caburetor will usually react in the same manner. It takes at least a half hour of running time for the parts to "bed in" properly. If the carburetor is still presenting problems after a half hour's running, hook the pressure tester up again and submerge the carburetor in a pan of water to determine the location of the leaks.

A pressure tester can also be used to test the operation of the carburetor metering diaphragm and inlet needle. Use the same hookup as before. Pump the gauge to 10 pounds per square inch. Use a pencil point on the carburetor metering diaphragm and depress it gently. If the carburetor is working properly in these areas, the gauge will immediately drop back to zero as the inlet needle is unseated. If the drop to zero doesn't occur, either the inlet mechanism is inoperative or the needle is stuck.

Whenever the carburetor is removed from the engine, you must use a new carburetor gasket to reassemble the engine. On two-stroke engines, the length of the fuel intake passage is critical. A gasket, no matter how sound it may appear to the eye, was crushed during its initial installation. Further compression will reduce it to less than critical size. This can make the carburetor difficult, or even impossible, to adjust for correct engine operation.

The Tillotson HU carburetor is similar to the Walbro HDC. What differences there are can be determined by carefully examining the carburetor and the exploded drawing in Fig. 5-3. To study the drawings and the carburetor before disassembly is a good idea when working with even the most familiar parts. But it absolutely essential to your success when the units are new to you.

Disassembly. Again, clean a disassembled carburetor in solvent and look for cracks and other signs of external body damage. Remove the idle speed screw assembly and check the assembly for signs of wear and damage. Next, inspect the idle speed screw threads in the carburetor body for damage or wear (these body threads are unlike the idle and high-speed circuit jet seats since a Heli-Coil repair kit is available from many dealers).

There are four screws holding the Tillotson carburetor body, fuel pump diaphragm, gasket and fuel pump cover casting together. Check the diaphragm for holes and make sure it's flat after removal if you are going to try to use it again. Also, check for possible leaks. Actually, the diaphragm is *recommended* for replacement, but the gasket *must* be replaced.

Continue to remove parts as indicated in the exploded view in Fig. 5-3 until you reach the metering diaphragm cover. Remove this cover and make a check of the metering diaphragm surface for holes, cracks, or other damage if it is not to be replaced.

Always remove and replace the gasket. Next, remove the fulcrum pin, inlet control lever, and inlet tension spring. The spring will be putting pressure on the inlet control lever, so care must be exercised when removing the pin. Under no circumstances should you stretch or bend this or any other carburetor spring. Such springs are made to manufacturer's specifications so the carburetor may be correctly adjusted. Any change will prevent you from bringing the carburetor into correct adjustment after the unit is reassembled.

Remove the inlet needle, the inlet needle seat assembly, and its gasket. In the Tillotson carburetor, the inlet seat can be changed if it has been damaged. If the change is made, the needle should be changed at the same time.

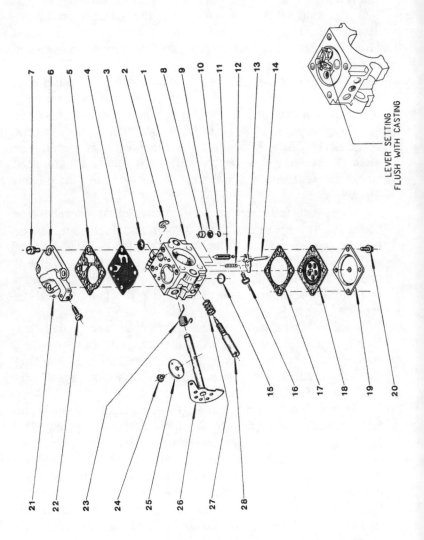

LEVER SETTING
FLUSH WITH CASTING

112

REF. NO.	NAME OF PART	REF. NO.	NAME OF PART
1	Carburetor Assembly Complete. .	15	Plug, 9/32 Dia. Welch . . . . .
2	"E" Ring	16	Screw, 4-40 x 5/16 Oval Hd. . .
3	Screen	17	Gasket, Metering Diaphragm . .
4	Diaphragm, Fuel Pump	18	Diaphgram Assembly . . . . . .
5	Gasket, Fuel Pump	19	Cover, Diaphragm . . . .
6	Cover, Pump	20	Screw & Lockwasher,
7	Screw & Lockwasher		4-40 x 1/4 RD. HD. . . . . .
	(6-32 x 5/16 FIL. HD.)	21	Ball 3/32 DIA Nylon . . . . . .
8	Cage, Main Fixed -	22	Screw, Idle Speed Regulating . .
	Orifice & Nozzle	23	Spring, Throttle Return . . . . .
9	Screen	24	Screw & Lockwasher,
10	Ring, Retainer		4-40 x 3/16 RD. HD. . . . . .
11	Needle, Inlet	25	Shutter, Throttle . . . .
12	Spring, Tension	26	Throttle Shaft & Lever Assy. . .
13	Lever, Inlet Control	27	Spring Adjusting Screw . . . . .
14	Pin, Fulcrum	28	Screw, Idle Adjustment . . . . .

Fig. 5-3. An exploded view of the Tillotson HU carburetor. (Courtesy Pioneer Chain Saws.)

113

Choke and throttle plate removal is very similar to that described for the Walbro; Remove the high speed and idle mixture screws and inspect them for wear or damage. Check for seat damage; even a tiny scratch will impair engine operation. If the seats are damaged, a new carburetor body will be needed. It's much simpler and probably cheaper to buy a new carburetor and save the time and effort of rebuilding. Choke and throttle plate removal is very similar to that described for the Walbro; check only if there is a very strong indication of wear in that area. If the shafts are checked for wear, the carburetor body must also be checked. If the body is worn, it must be replaced. If the shaft is worn, and the body is not, the shaft must be replaced; the body can be retained.

Assembly. When reinstalling the seat and needle, make sure all parts are totally clean, use a new gasket, and torque the assembly to 25 inch-pounds. This exchange should never be attempted without a torque wrench because the torque setting is critical. Next, install the inlet tension spring, the inlet control lever, the fulcrum pin, and the fulcrum pin retaining screw. Make sure the inlet control lever rotates freely on the fulcrum pin. There should be no binding at all.

Adjust the inlet control lever so that its center, where it contacts the metering diaphragm, will be flush with the metering chamber floor. Place the diaphragm body casting over the diaphragm and its new gasket and secure it to the main carburetor assembly.

The fuel pump gasket is placed in the pump cover, then the fuel pump diaphragm is placed next to the gasket. This is done so that the flap valves will seat against the fuel pump cover. Any other order can prevent that seating. Install the fuel pump cover and attach with screws.

Install the high speed mixture screw and the idle mixture screw. Idle bypass holes should be inspected for plugging. If plugging is present, the holes must be cleaned with compressed air. To try to poke a wire through the holes may change their flow characteristics.

Fig. 5-4 shows a Tillotson HS carburetor for comparison purposes. There are great similarities and only small differences, overall, but these small differences are very important. Carefully review any available carburetor parts drawings when getting ready to do a rebuild.

Carburetor Servicing Tips

Use a small magnifying glass to inspect the tips of high- and low-speed needles and their seats in the carburetor body. Any scratching or wear evident under slight magnification means the needles must be replaced for proper operation; scoring and scratching at a seat requires complete carburetor body replacement.

When removing the needle valve assembly on a carburetor, you'll find a small hexagonal section. Use the proper size small socket on this section; never use a screwdriver.

When checking the throttle and choke shaft assemblies on any small carburetor, move the shafts back and forth to check for binding. Move them throughout their full range. If the shafts bind, apply solvent and retest. If they are not free, remove and replace worn parts as needed

Many small carburetors use a device called a welch plug to cover holes (manufacturing is a few cents cheaper when the mold can be made with a few extra holes at certain spots). These spots and their plugs have a tendency to interfere with carburetor cleaning and can eventually develop leaks. In new carburetors, there's really not much point in removing and replacing welch plugs. But if the plugs leak and interfere with cleaning, there are two methods of removal and one of installation.

Method one requires a small chisel to pierce the plug. The chisel should be 1/8 inch in width or a bit less. Exercise caution to avoid damaging the carburetor body when piercing a welch plug. After the plug is pierced, a gentle prying action will lift it out.

Method number two requires more care and is probably not the best for the amateur mechanic. A flat punch about half the size of the welch plug is placed in its center. The punch is then driven into the plug which should then come right out. Again, care must be used to not strike the carburetor body. A major problem is the possibility of a welch plug being driven into the carburetor body should the flat punch be struck with too hard a blow.

Installation on the other hand is simple. A new welch plug is set into the carburetor body; it will ride a bit above the channel reducer, or shoulder, under the hole. A flat-end punch the same size or just a bit larger than the welch plug is placed

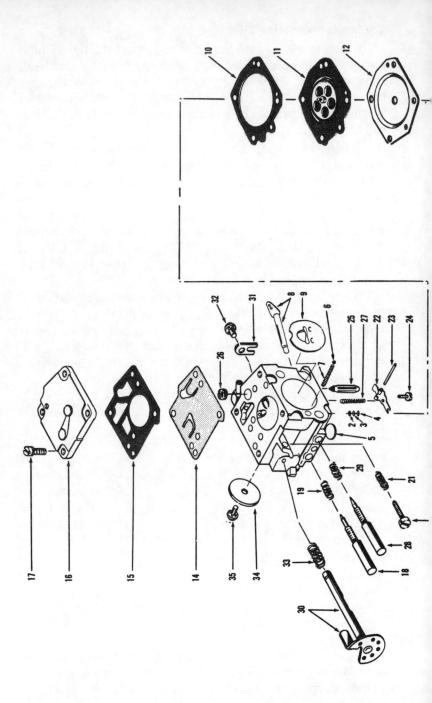

REF. NO.	QTY. PER ASSY.	NAME OF PART
1	1	Carburetor Complete
2	1	Body Channel Screen
3	1	Body Channel Screen Ret. Ring
4	1	Body Channel Welch Plug (small)
5	1	Body Channel Welch Plug (large)
6	1	Choke Friction Ball
7	1	Choke Friction Spring
8	1	Choke Shaft & Lever
9	1	Choke Shutter
10	1	Diaphragm Cover
11	1	Diaphragm
12	1	Diaphragm Cover
13	4	Diaphragm Cover Ret. Screw & L'washer
14	1	Fuel Pump Diaphragm
15	1	Fuel Pump Gasket
16	1	Fuel Pump Cover
17	4	Fuel Pump Cover Ret. Screw & L'washer
18	1	Idle Mixture Screw
19	1	Idle Mixture Screw Spring
20	1	Idle Speed Screw
21	1	Idle Speed Screw Spring
22	1	Inlet Control Lever
23	1	Inlet Pinion Pin
24	1	Inlet Pinion Pin Ret. Screw
25	1	Inlet Needle
26	1	Inlet Screen
27	1	Inlet Tension Spring
28	1	High Speed Mixture Screw
29	1	High Speed Mixture Screw Spring
30	4	Throttle Shaft & Lever
31	1	Throttle Shaft Clip
32	1	Throttle Shaft Clip Ret. Screw
33	1	Throttle Shaft Return Spring
34	1	Throttle Shutter
35	4	Throttle Shutter Screw

Fig. 5-4. An exploded view of a Tillotson HS carburetor. (Courtesy Pioneer Chain Saws.)

on the plug's surface and tapped. Don't use enough power to dent the plug, and especially don't use enough power to drive it into the carburetor body. A coating of clear shellac will help seal the new plug.

In Walbro carburetors, the main jet should not be removed for carburetor cleaning unless you've already obtained a correct replacement (the type with an undercut groove). This is because the factory cross drills the main jet which, once removed from the carburetor body, cannot be realigned.

Carburetor gasket surfaces should be checked for flatness before reassembly, as shown in Fig. 5-5. Use a machinist's rule and a 0.002 inch flat feeler gauge. If you can slide the 0.002 inch feeler gauge under a rule laid across the gasket surfaces, it is an indication that the surface is warped and the gasket will have a difficult time sealing properly. Replace the warped-surface part or try a nonhardening gasket sealer such as Permatex Aviation Gasket Sealer.

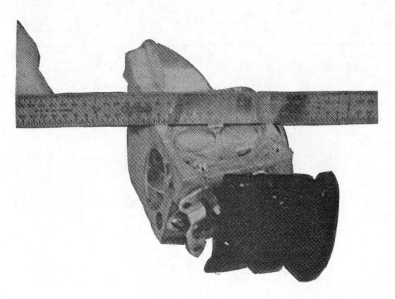

Fig. 5-5. Checking the flatness of gasket surfaces. (Courtesy McCulloch.)

When reinstalling the carburetor, use the machinist's ruler and the 0.002 inch feeler gauge again. If the surface on which the carburetor is mounted is warped, use General Electric Hi-Temp gasket material to coat the warped side of the gasket.

Some people recommend using two gaskets, but with most two-stroke engines, even a fraction of an inch in extra inlet passage length can drastically affect engine operation. Don't use standard gasket sealer either, for this will eventually cause problems (nonhardening or not, standard gasket sealer does harden in time).

CLUTCH SERVICING

Clutch replacement does not require highly specialized tools, though at least one tool, the spanner, is needed. I will cover clutches for direct drive chain saw models only, since gear-driven chain saws are usually intended for professional use.

The spanner, or rotor removal tool, will usually be needed to replace chain saw clutches. The cost of the spanner is usually reasonable, and it is best to buy through the dealer who sells your brand of saw.

Fig. 5-6. The spanner is bolted to the clutch rotor. (Courtesy Homelite.)

The spanner (Fig. 5-6) has a hole that fits over the rotor nut, with bolts that set into holes in the clutch rotor. The spanner prevents the rotor from turning as you turn the rotor nut, or screw, to free the clutch drum.

To make a spanner, use a piece of 1/4 inch thick steel twice as wide as the rotor nut. Drill a hole for the rotor nut, and two other holes spaced to fit the holes in the rotor. Insert two bolts of the correct size and the spanner is ready to use (Fig. 5-7).

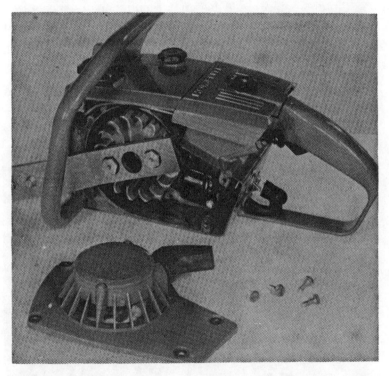

Fig. 5-7. Three holes in a piece of 1/4 inch steel can make a very effective spanner. (Courtesy Homelite.)

The spanner can be replaced by an oil filter wrench, though you should make sure it is a heavy duty model. The light filter wrenches may break apart with the amount of torque applied to the rotor nut. If a chain style filter wrench is used, it is essential that you wrap the rotor with several layers of rag to keep from chipping, scoring, or cracking the lighter metal of the rotor.

Once the spanner or filter wrench is in place, you must check to see whether the rotor has a left- or right-hand thread.

Fig. 5-8. Make sure the space between the hub and the friction material is equal all around. (Courtesy Homelite.)

Since left-hand threads are more common, try this first. Set the correct size socket wrench on the rotor nut and turn clockwise. If the nut doesn't spin off, you have a right-hand thread and must reverse the turning to loosen the nut.

Once the rotor nut is backed off a few turns, it will spin off by hand. The rotor, or clutch friction hub, can now be pulled loose by hand. Turn the hub inside the clutch drum to check for any wobble that will show uneven wear of the friction material. The gap between the friction material and the hub should look even all the way around the clutch (Fig. 5-8). If the clutch has been slipping too much or the chain has been engaging while the engine runs at a slow idle, the clutch contact surfaces may be burned or badly worn, the clutch drum may be out of round, or the clutch bearing may be out of round. This bearing should be lubricated at least once every 100 hours of operation. If the bearing is dry or worn out (Fig. 5-9) check the crankshaft end where the bearing rides. This

Fig. 5-9. Check the bearing and the crankshaft end where the bearing rides. (Courtesy Homelite.)

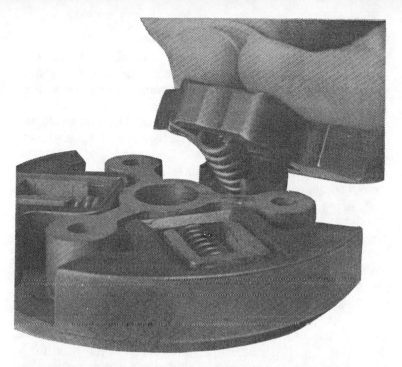

Fig. 5-10. Put one end of the spring in the spring compartment, barely catch the shoe over the back of the compartment, and place the other end of the spring in contact with the inside edge of the shoe. Then push down with both thumbs to snap the spring and shoe into place. (Courtesy Homelite.)

shaft end can become worn if operation with a dry or worn-out bearing goes on for too long or if operation with too loose a clutch is continued for an excessive period of time.

As the illustration shows, the drive sprocket is attached to the clutch drum. If this sprocket shows signs of gouges, sharpened teeth, cracks, or other major wear or damage, replace it.

Clutch shoes and springs can be replaced by lifting at the hub and pulling the shoe and spring out, as shown in Fig. 5-10. The replacement is a simple reversal of the removal procedure. A complete breakdown of parts is shown in Fig. 5-11.

Caution: Some clutch shoes contain asbestos. It has been shown that asbestos dust is carcinogenic. So be careful not to breathe the dust when working with the clutch shoes.

ENGINE TEARDOWNS AND REBUILDS

Because of the structural simplicity of the two-stroke engine, the average person can easily do teardowns and almost total engine rebuilds at home, using very few specialized tools.

In many cases, the only two tools needed that we would not expect to find in the homeowner's toolbox are a torque wrench indicating in both inch-pounds and foot-pounds and an impact driver, or impact wrench, with a selection of tips. Of course, the old standard tools are still needed: a set of sockets for 3/8 inch drive ratchet handles, a set of screwdrivers, both standard and Phillips, the spanner for clutch and rotor removal, various small tools including a set of box and open end wrenches, pliers, and locking pliers. Also, a set of metric tools is becoming essential as the U.S. makes its conversion to get in step with the rest of the world.

Recommending one toolmaker over another is often unfair. I'm not going to tell you to select a Poulan over a Pioneer. Besides, the tool that fits my hand may not fit yours very well. But I can honestly state there is little need for a home mechanic, no matter how skilled and willing he may be, to purchase the most costly top-of-the-line tools. Staying with solid, reputable brands is essential, of course, but there's no need to pay $6 for a wrench that a $3 one can replace in every respect except longevity under daily, heavy use. Look to Craftsman (Sears), Crescent, Husky, Mac, S & K, and a wide

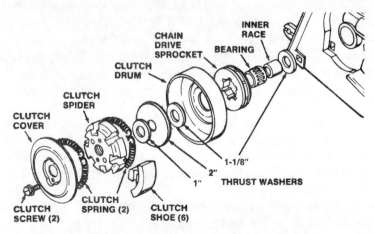

Fig. 5-11. A typical chain saw clutch assembly. (Courtesy Homelite.)

range of other makers for a suitable line of tools; many are even guaranteed for as long as you own them.

From the top down, your chain saw engine is simple to tear down. Some chain saw two-strokes use a single casting cylinder barrel that also includes the cylinder head. These units lift directly off the piston and must be replaced as a unit. Others (and there seem to be fewer and fewer all the time) use the two-part cylinder head and cylinder barrel system. The two-part system is somewhat easier to work with for some operations, so it is generally a bit easier to repair.

As usual, there are advantages and disadvantages to each system. First, the one-piece cylinder head engine cannot suffer from a warped cylinder head, though it can still be seated improperly on the lower engine cases. While a two-piece unit, in contrast, does offer some slight chance of cylinder head warpage, particularly if it is not torqued down correctly. Other problems are as easily corrected, and the cylinder, if worn out, can be replaced more cheaply because it is a smaller and simpler casting. Although piston installation is usually easier when replacing piston rings with the separate cylinder head units, someone who tears down enough of the one-piece cylinders will quickly develop a knack for sneaking things into place without ruining anything.

The literature that comes with your chain saw will probably give absolutely no information on whether or not the engine's top end is a one- or two-piece unit. Your dealer should know.

Some of the readily available one-piece units now on the market are: Homelite's entire EZ series, their XL series, including the XL 12 and the XL Mini, the 150 Automatic, the XL 2; Jonsenreds Lil-Jon 50 and most other Jonsenreds; McCulloch's Mac 15, Mini-Mac and 6, and the Power Mac 6; Partner; Pioneer's P20, P25, P40; Remington; Skil; Roper; Echo (which includes some of the newer Sears Craftsman saws); Lombards; Solo; Stihl; Poulan. In those with no models listed, all or nearly all the saws use single-unit cylinder construction, a fact that surely demonstrates the favorable position this type of engine holds in the industry. For a look at the breakdown of a one-piece cylinder head engine, see the exploded drawing and parts list in Fig. 5-12.

Upper End Teardown and Rebuild

The following is the general teardown procedure. Certain steps may differ slightly for your particular chain saw.

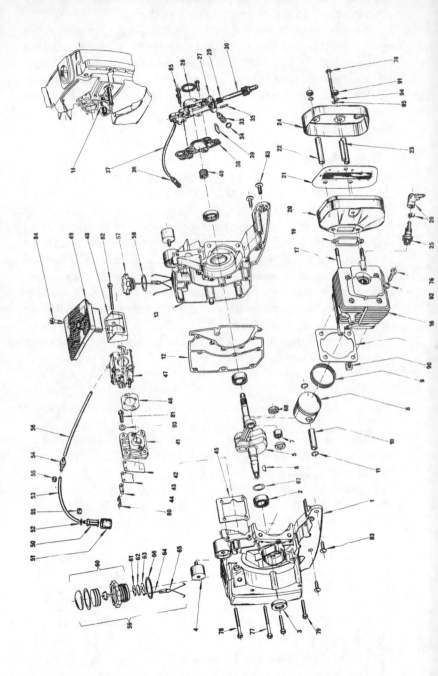

126

PIONEER MODEL P40

REF. NO.	NAME OF PART	REF. NO.	NAME OF PART	REF. NO.	NAME OF PART
1	Crankcase Half, blower side	28	Felt Seal	58	O-Ring, oil cap
2	Main Bearing	29	Spring, plunger	59	Gas Cap assy.
3	Seal	30	Plunger assy.	60	Gas Cap Body assy.
4	Shock Absorber	33	Adjusting Screw, oil pump	61	Cover Plate, gas cap
5	C'Shaft & Con. Rod Ass'y. (includes 1 pc item No.2 & item No. 67)	34	O-Ring - oil pump	62	Filter Disc, gas cap
6	Key, flywheel	35	Spirol Pin, oil pump	63	Cover, gas cap
7	Bearing, wrist pin	36	Oil Pickup Head assy.	64	Bead Chain, gas cap
8	Piston & Dow Pin assy.	37	Oil Hose	65	Spring, gas cap
9	Piston Ring Set	38	Gasket, oil pump	66	O-Ring, gas cap
10	Wrist Pin	39	Seal, oil pump	67	Washer - Thrust Face
11	Retainer, wrist pin	40	Worm, oil pump	68	Thrust Washer, wrist pin
12	Gasket, crankcase	41	Reed Valve assy.	76	Screw, cylinder
13	Crankcase Half, mag. side	42	Reed	77	Screw, crankcase
14	Groove Pin	43	Reed Stiffener	78	Screw, crankcase
		44	Retainer Plate, reed		Muffler
16	Cylinder	45	Gasket, reed to crankcase	79	Screw, crankcase
17	Stud, cylinder	46	Gasket, carburetor to reed	80	Screw, reed valve
18	Gasket, cylinder	47	Carburetor Complete	81	Screw, reed body to crankcase
19	Gasket, muffler	48	Elbow, air filter	82	Screw, reed body to carburetor
20	Muffler Body assy.	49	Air Filter incl. item No. 84	83	Screw, shock absorber
21	Baffle Plate assy., muffler	50	Fuel Pickup assy.	84	Screw, air filter to elbow
22	Spacer, muffler	51	Filter Felt, fuel pickup	85	Screw, oil pump
23	Spacer, muffler	52	Washer, fuel pickup	90	Nut, cylinder
24	Cover, muffler	53	Fuel Hose, connector to pickup	91	Nut, muffler
25	Spark Plug	54	Fuel Connector Assy.	92	Washer, cylinder
26	Sparky Cover assy.	55	Speed Clip, fuel pickup	93	Washer, reed body
*	Oil Pump assy. complete	56	Fuel Hose, carburetor to pickup	94	Lockwasher, muffler
27	Oil Pump Body assy.	57	Oil Cap assy.	95	Lockwasher, muffler

* NOT SHOWN

Fig. 5-12. A one-piece cylinder head chain saw engine. (Courtesy Pioneer Chain Saws.)

The first job in getting ready to tear down any chain saw engine is to remove the guide bar and chain. Next, the muffler and air filters are removed and put aside. Any gas in the tank should be emptied by this time so the saw can be turned around and carburetor connections taken loose without slopping fuel all over the work area. See Fig. 5-13.

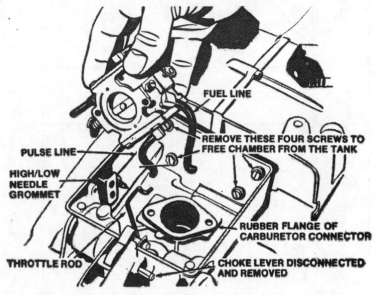

Fig. 5-13. Disassembling a chain saw engine. (Courtesy Homelite.)

Now remove the air cleaner bracket screw and use a pair of needlenose pliers to remove the cotter pin that holds the choke linkage to the choke plate link.

Move up to the saw's handle with a screwdriver and remove the section covering the throttle trigger linkage. Pull the cotter pin joining the linkage (some types of triggers may have links other than cotter pins, but almost all can be easily removed with a pair of needlenose pliers and a screwdriver).

Using an open end wrench (or a box wrench if it will fit), remove the retaining screws holding the carburetor to the cylinder. The carburetor can now be set aside.

Next, the starter and flywheel cover side screws are removed from the chain saw housing. The starter and side cover will lift away together on most saws, exposing the flywheel. This housing unit can be set aside or repaired as needed. See Fig. 5-14.

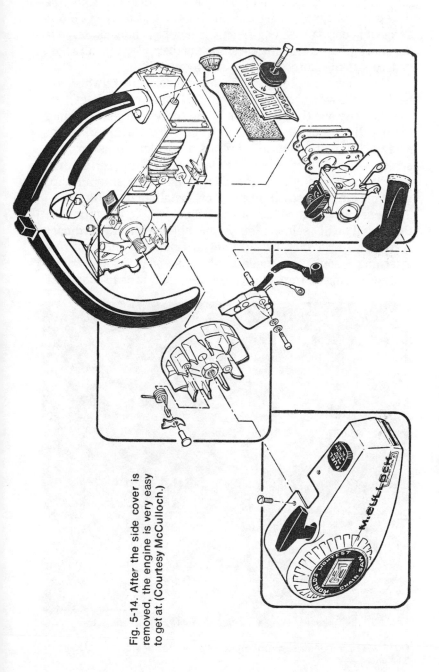

Fig. 5-14. After the side cover is removed, the engine is very easy to get at. (Courtesy McCulloch.)

For further removal of the engine, use your needlenose pliers and reach in to pull out the wire terminal from the magneto kill switch. Any oiler lines attached directly to any accessible parts of the engine should now be removed. Remove the spark plug. There may well be another oiler line attached underneath the clutch. Disconnect any such fitting.

Flywheel side plates on the upper side of the flywheel are held in place with screws. Unscrew and remove the plates.

Now remove the engine mounting screws. In some engines these will be slot-head screws, while others will be Phillips screws. Homelite generally prefers a type known as Pozidriv screws which, though closely resembling Phillips head screws, are different enough to get chewed up badly if a Phillips screwdriver is used to remove or install them (Fig. 5-15). These screws, regardless of their type, will be exceptionally tight and will seldom be removable with an ordinary screwdriver. In fact, no attempt at final tightening or first loosening should be made with a standard screwdriver. Consider using an impact screwdriver and a 12 or 16 ounce ball

Fig. 5-15. Some engine mounting screws are Pozidriv screws. (Courtesy Homelite.)

peen hammer to loosen (and later to tighten) the engine mounting screws.

On many saws, a smaller screw holds the rear part of the housing to the bottom of the housing. Remove this with a standard screwdriver of the correct size. You should now be able to lift off the rear part of the housing. This unfortunately usually destroys the gasket sealing the reed plate to the housing. Keep a full set of gaskets on hand while operating on the internals of any engine. They're cheap enough. The engine can now be lifted the rest of the way out of the casing. See Fig. 5-16.

Fig. 5-16. A chain saw engine out of its casing. (Courtesy Solo.)

If the engine is a reed-valve type, the reed-valve can now be pulled out, after removing the screws holding it in, as shown in Fig. 5-17. Unbolt the four cylinder head (or cylinder) nuts and wiggle the cylinder gently until it will slide easily off the piston.

You have now performed an upper end teardown and are ready to get on with the removal of the piston rings and wrist

Fig. 5-17. Removing the reed valve. (Courtesy Homelite.)

pin, which are usually the major reason for a teardown job anyway.

Borrowing or renting a set of micrometers would be a good idea at this point. If piston removal is needed, now is the time for new piston rings. Anytime the piston is removed, new piston rings are a good idea because the removal is almost certain to scuff the rings. Before installing the new piston rings, though, you should check both piston and cylinder bore for damage.

First, examine the surfaces of the piston carefully, looking for evidence of scuffing or scoring. Generally, a piston that has been scuffed or scored *above* the piston pin indicates excessive overheating. Among the causes of overheating are an overly lean fuel mixture, too little oil in the fuel mix, the wrong kind of oil in the fuel mix, air leaks in the carburetor, damaged cooling fins, blow-by at damaged piston rings, or excessive carbon buildup in the engine.

If the piston is scuffed or scored *below* the piston pin, it is probably caused by either insufficient lubrication or a poor piston fit in the cylinder bore. If the piston is scuffed, scored, or otherwise damaged in any way, it must be replaced. When a piston is replaced, the piston pin and any plugs holding the piston pin in place must also be replaced.

Checking the cylinder bore will indicate whether or not there has been severe enough scuffing to cause metal transfer to the cylinder wall. In a few cases, the cylinder walls may also be scored, but there should be few cases of this since most modern chain saw cylinder bores are chrome plated. Cast iron cylinder linings, unlike chrome, can easily be honed or rebored. Always be sure to match cylinder size to piston size. If the cylinder is rebored, or honed heavily, use the correct oversize piston and the proper size rings for the new piston.

Any newly honed cylinder should be washed with soap and water. Because most solvents won't remove all the abrasive used in the honing process, a thorough washing is essential, but so is immediate and correct lubrication of the cylinder walls. The use of a blower-type hair dryer can dry the cylinder walls rapidly enough to prevent any rusting. Since only the cast iron cylinder walls react well to honing and reboring, rust can be a real problem if not prevented at the outset.

The piston may suffer from other problems too. Carbon buildup in ring grooves should always be cleared out. Check the groove for nicks, both before and after carbon removal. If the lands (the area between the piston ring grooves) are bent or broken, replace the piston. If the grooves show stepped wear after the rings are removed, replace the piston. If there are nicks in the groove, they will also force piston replacement. Of course, any damage to the piston skirt or crown will also require replacement of the piston.

In most cases, ring side clearance in small chain saw engines will be about 0.002 to 0.003 inches. If the ring clearance exceeds this figure, there will be a loss of power and other problems. If the rings are tighter than the lower figure, the engine runs a very real chance of seizing early during its overhauled life. Use a flat feeler gauge to measure ring side clearance.

Ring end clearance varies widely for different engines even with the same manufacturer, so this figure must be checked out with a dealer or other service shop.

Usually no measurement of the cylinder bore will be needed. If the bore is hard chrome plated, replace when the plating wears enough to expose the base metal of the casting.

Cast iron cylinders can be honed, or rebored as needed, up to a maximum overbore recommended by the manufacturer. Check the piston sizes the manufacturer offers; the largest oversize piston offered will be the maximum recommended overbore. A glaze-breaking hone should be used in a cast iron cylinder anytime an overhaul is done, and the cylinder should then be measured with an inside micrometer to determine whether or not an oversize piston and piston rings are needed. If stock piston rings exceed about 0.004 inches in side clearance, the next size piston will be needed. You will probably have to rebore the cylinder to make the new piston fit. This, however, is a job not adaptable to home workshops, and, in fact, one not ever undertaken by most dealers. You can probably contract to have it done through your dealer, or you locate a machine shop with the correct size boring bar for your engine.

When the piston is replaced, the wrist pin, or piston pin, must be driven out (Fig. 5-18). Special drivers are available for this job, but in almost every case, a metal rod (smaller in diameter than the wrist pin and about 2 inches longer overall) will do the job just as well. Piston pins are held in place by several different types of fasteners. Some are plastic plugs, and on these you may need the manufacturer's tool to remove the pin without damaging things. Others use snap rings which can easily be removed with needlenose pliers.

To reinstall the piston in the cylinder, a piston ring compressor is almost essential. The job can be done without the compressor, but it's a sure bet you'll end up with a new vocabulary—suitable for use around mule skinners only. Since a piston ring compressor costs under $5, getting one seems the most sensible way to go (Fig. 5-19).

Use new gaskets when installing the cylinder on the lower end. Make sure the surfaces are completely clear of all old gasket material and gasket cement and use a nonhardening gasket sealer to help prevent leaks.

Next, clean all gasket cement, rust, and other debris off any screw, nut, or stud being torqued down. All such trash can, and will, cause false torque readings. Next, provide a light coat of lubrication, usually a lightweight oil. If some other type of lubrication is specified with a definite torque value, then use that lubrication and no other; different types of lubricant can cause a difference of more than 100 percent in indicated torque

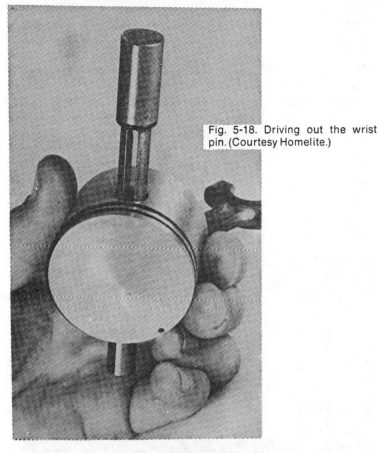

Fig. 5-18. Driving out the wrist pin. (Courtesy Homelite.)

readings. Overtorquing is especially hard on bolts and nuts of the size used on chain saw engines. Run the nuts or bolts down finger tight and use a wrench to make a few more turns.

When using the torque wrench, follow the manufacturer's diagram for multifastener installations. If none is provided, move on a diagonal. Do a corner bolt or nut, then move to the opposite corner, and so on, across the part being torqued down. Bring the first fastener to about 70 percent of its final torque value, then move on to each fastener in proper sequence and tighten each to the same value.

A fastener cannot be checked for applied torque once it has been tightened, so care must be used for the last 10 percent tightening, and many people personally prefer to increment in steps of 5 percent. If there is any doubt as to the correctness of applied torque, use a wrench to back off the fastener from one-half to one full turn and then use the torque wrench to bring it back to specifications.

Lower End Teardown and Rebuild

If the lower end seems in need of repairs, the basic recommendation for most people is simply to take the thing to the dealer. Though piston ring, piston, and piston pin replacement are reasonably simple, lower end work on any engine is a lot more complex, needs a greater number of parts, and a wider assortment of tools, often special tools available from only a few makers. For those who already have some engine rebuilding experience though, the rebuilding of an engine can be a moneysaver as well as an enjoyable way to spend some time.

Fig. 5-19. Compress the piston rings in the ring grooves with a piston ring compressor. (Courtesy Homelite.)

Because of the wide variation in bearing style and engine design, I will present a general overview of bottom end rebuild techniques. To provide a starting point, we'll look at a teardown and reassembly of a Homelite 150 Automatic. Disassembly is reasonably simple with this engine and begins with clearing away the bar, chain, tanks, and so forth, as done in preparation for upper end teardowns.

When the engine is down to its "short block" configuration, that is, just the cylinder and crankcase assembly, open the engine by removing the two hex head screws which run through the cylinder flange. Next, remove the two hex head screws on the oil reservoir side of the crankcase. Now, maintain a tight grip on the crankcase and pull the cylinder away.

At this point, the piston, rod, and crankshaft assembly can easily be lifted out of the crankcase. Homelite recommends complete replacement of the following parts: thrust bearings, main roller bearings, rubber seals and needle bearings, and the connecting rod cap at the crankthrow.

Perform all the normal upper end checks for piston and cylinder wear and scoring, as discussed earlier. Now, check the wrist pin bearings. If they are worn flat or can be separated by more than the width of a single needle, the bearing should be replaced. But here, special tools are needed. First, a fixture to provide support for the bearing to be pressed out—such as a steel plate with a hole large enough to pass the

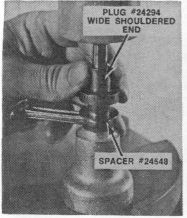

Fig. 5-20. Homelite's special plug and spacer can be used with an arbor press to push out the old bearing of a connecting rod.

bearing. If the old bearing is damaged or worn, you don't care what happens to it, but installing the new bearing properly avoids premature damage. Homelite makes a special tool, plug No. 24294, and a spacer No. 24548, that will, in use with an arbor press, press the old bearing out and the new one in as shown in Fig. 5-20. Most other manufacturers have similar tools available, and most dealers are happy to sell them to you. The old bearing is pressed out with the wide-shouldered end of the plug, while the new bearing is pressed in with the narrow end, plus the spacer. The spacer makes certain the bearing sinks into the bore to the correct depth.

Now the crankshaft, connecting rod, and piston parts should be laid out in their correct assembly relationships, as shown in Fig. 5-21, and assembled as follows:

1. Install the connecting rod on the piston by pressing the piston pin, closed end first, from the intake side (intake side has two piston ring locating pins) of the piston.
2. The connecting rod must be assembled to the crankpin journal so that the mating pips of the connecting rod are paired as shown in Fig. 5-22. If the assembly is not mated, the rod will not fit.
3. The intake side of the piston (the side on which the open ends of the piston rings butt against the locating pins) must be toward the intake side of the engine (the intake side of the engine is also the magneto side of the engine).

No binding roughness is permissible when the needle bearings are assembled. Complete freedom of movement is needed. Connecting rod cap screws should be tightened to a minimum of 60 inch-pounds of torque. This is an essential procedure, for any major torque variation will cause premature engine failure.

When the crankshaft and rod are assembled, move on to the crankcase. Remove the old seals and bearings and replace them with new parts. The open side of the seals go towards the inside of the engine. Crankshaft retaining rings are placed in their ring grooves by positioning the split end downward and pressing till they are fastened in placed.

No cylinder gasket is used on this engine, but the sealing surfaces of the crankcase were coated with a film of GE RTV

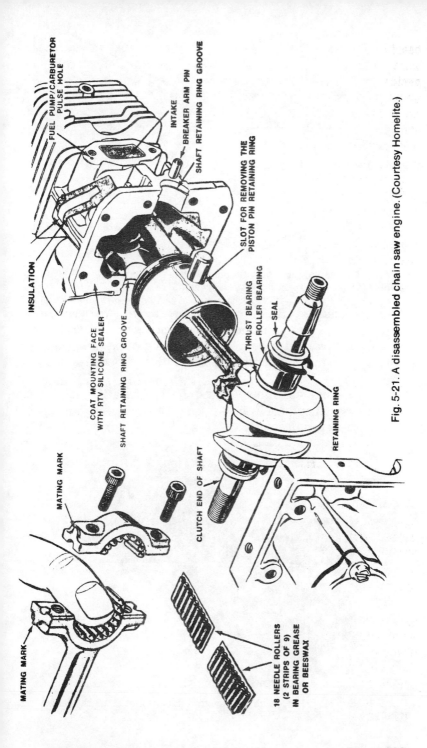

FUEL PUMP/CARBURETOR PULSE HOLE

INTAKE

BREAKER ARM PIN

SHAFT RETAINING RING GROOVE

INSULATION

SLOT FOR REMOVING THE PISTON PIN RETAINING RING

COAT MOUNTING FACE WITH RTV SILICONE SEALER

SHAFT RETAINING RING GROOVE

THRUST BEARING

ROLLER BEARING

SEAL

MATING MARK

MATING MARK

CLUTCH END OF SHAFT

RETAINING RING

MATING MARK

18 NEEDLE ROLLERS (2 STRIPS OF 9) IN BEARING GREASE OR BEESWAX

Fig. 5-21. A disassembled chain saw engine. (Courtesy Homelite.)

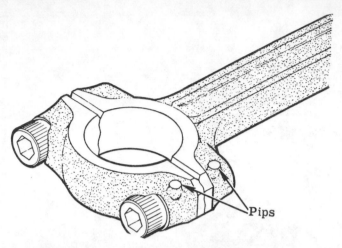

Fig. 5-22. The mating pips must be paired when the connecting rod is assembled to the crankpin. (Courtesy McCulloch.)

silicone sealant (RTV stands for room temperature vulcanizing). Clean all the old sealant from the sealing surfaces and spread a very thin, smooth coating of silicone sealant over them in preparation for final assembly (Fig. 5-23).

Before final assembly, check the crankshaft seals for straightness. They should be as square to the crankshaft as possible to prevent leakage.

Fig. 5-23. Sealing surfaces covered with a thin coat of silicone sealant. (Courtesy McCulloch.)

The crankshaft *must* remain aligned with the crankshaft journals at all times during final assembly. If the piston and crankshaft deviate as little as 5 degrees from their correct position, the piston rings will expand into the ports and will snap when the assembly is straightened.

Make sure the piston ring ends are located at the retaining pins, then you can squirt some oil onto the cylinder walls. Next, push the piston down into the cylinder using a piston ring compressor. Check again to make certain nothing has slipped out of place or become cocked inside the crankcase. This will be your last chance to check things over and correct any mistakes.

Align the cylinder with the crankcase, fit them together, and use the following tightening procedure. Install the four sets of flat washers and the socket-head cap screws; tighten them alternately until a final torque reading of 40 inch pounds is reached.

Apply Loctite to the two hex-head washer head screws and install them in the bottom holes of the cylinder mounting flange. These screws are tightened to 36 inch-pounds. There are four more hex-head washer head screws that go through the crankcase to the oil tank; these are installed when the tank is being assembled to the crankcase.

And that about covers one engine teardown. Not really particularly difficult, but still a job that requires an arbor press and some other specialized tools. While the tool expense may not seem great, there's little chance the plug and spacer will be used more than a single time for most homeowners. And the job is sensitive. One mistake is all it will take to present you with a pile of junk when the rebuilt engine is started. Care and patience are essential.

McCulloch's engines are also fairly easy to tear down. First, as always, the saw is taken down so the engine can be removed from the powerhead. Then the four screws holding the crankcase bottom to the cylinder are removed, and the bottom is pulled away from the cylinder. The crankshaft, connecting rod, and piston can then be easily lifted out as an assembled unit.

If the clutch rotor has been removed, the oil seals, retaining rings, crankshaft bearings, and thrust plate can then be pulled out. The two connecting rod screws are removed and the rod and piston are lifted off the crankshaft. McCulloch recommends reinstalling the rod cap on the rod so that it can't get lost. The piston and piston rings are inspected and cared for with the same procedure described earlier in this chapter. McCulloch says that a holding block, guide, driver, and drift pin are needed for upper end work.

Use a sieve for small parts such as bearings. Dip all parts in solvent and make sure they're as clean as possible. Dry them with compressed air. If you have no source of air pressure, most camera stores carry at least one brand of "canned" air for cleaning negatives; however, the stuff does tend to be very expensive for this sort of use. Also, there are air tanks available in 3 1/2 and 7 cubic foot capacities, with air spray attachments; these are easy to locate, for most motorcycle shops specializing in dirt bikes can either sell you one off the shelf or order one for you. Generally, the smaller tanks are under $20 and can be filled at any service station.

Clean all interior parts, using commercial carburetor cleaner to loosen up the heavier carbon deposits not removed with standard solvents. Inspect the crankcase for cracks or damaged surfaces inside and out. Check screw holes for stripped thread. Most stripped threads can be repaired with Heli Coil insert kits.

Check crankshaft bearing surfaces for scoring or wear. Check for a broken flywheel keyway. Look for any broken or damaged threads at each end of the crankshaft. Minor burring around the keyway can be removed with a fine file and a finish dressing with crocus cloth, but major damage or uneven wear anywhere in this area is a sign that the part needs replacing.

Place the crankshaft bearings on the shaft and spin them by hand to check for any binding or roughness. Replace all bearings and oil seals during the rebuild.

Go through the mounting of rings and piston pins, etc., and then coat the inside of the cylinder with a soupy mixture of SAE 30 oil and a nonabrasive, kitchen cleanser. You might try Bon Ami for this job. Insert the piston, with its new rings, in the bore and run the piston up and down by hand for about 5 minutes. When the rings are polished and mated to the cylinder bore, remove the piston, thoroughly clean the rings, and blow the assembly dry with low air pressure. Then coat the piston with SAE 30 oil, clean the cylinder, and coat it with the same oil. This procedure eliminates most of the long breakin time for chromed piston rings and cylinder walls, and it can be used with almost any hard-plated piston and cylinder. But it is essential that you remove all the cleaning compound before the final assembly. Otherwise, wear will rapidly accelerate past the breakin stage and result in a premature power loss or failure.

After the pre-break-in procedure is completed, the crankshaft is ready for installation. Align the pips on the rod and its cap. If the pips, or mating marks, don't align, the rod will not fit. Almost all small chain saw engines use connecting rods and rod caps that have been cracked along a natural fracture line; thus, a rod will only fit the cap from which it was originally broken. Pips must mate, or the rod must be replaced.

McCulloch's Power Mac 6 uses 20 rollers inside the connecting rod. Coat the inner surfaces of the rod and cap with grease and place 10 rollers on each surface. Make absolutely certain all 20 rollers are used!

Place the connecting rod on the crankshaft, add the cap, and install the screws (Fig. 5-24). Tighten the screws to 35 or

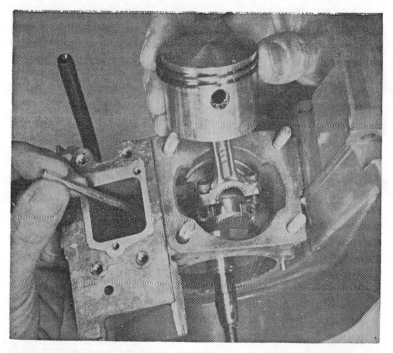

Fig. 5-24. Installing the connecting rod on the crankshaft. (Courtesy Homelite.)

40 inch-pounds after making sure no rollers fell out of the grease during installation. Finally, move the rod around the crankshaft by hand to check for roughness or binding.

Now give all the crankshaft bearing surfaces a light coat of SAE 30 oil. Place the thrust plates on the crankshaft, aligning the chamfered side of the thrust plates against the crankshaft throw, as shown in Fig. 5-25.

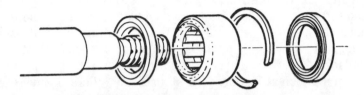

Fig. 5-25. When putting the thrust plates on the crankshaft, insure that the chamfered side of the thrust plates go next to the crankshaft throw. (Courtesy McCulloch.)

Lightly coat the oil seals with a lightweight auto chassis grease (not a cup grease). Put the oil seals on the crankshaft with the open side of the seals against the retaining rings. Line up and connect the assembled piston to the crankshaft so that the flywheel end of the shaft is on the opposite side of the cylinder from the exhaust port.

Insert the piston in the cylinder bore using a ring compressor. Seat the crankshaft on the bearing surface of the cylinder. The open portion of each retaining ring must be seated in the ring grooves in the cylinder base before the crankcase bottom section is placed on the assembly. The side marked flywheel must be on the flywheel side of the assembly. Make sure the retaining rings are fitting into their grooves as the unit is assembled.

Use a drop of Loctite or Permalock on each of the allen head screws and torque them to 45 to 50 inch pounds. Turn the crankshaft by hand a few times to check for any binding, rubbing, or hitting. If everything is moving smoothly, the unit can be reinstalled in the powerhead, and the rest of the saw can be assembled.

As you can see, there's not a lot of difference between the McCulloch and Homelite lower end jobs as far as actual assembly work goes. Torque values, the exact layout of parts, and other specifics will differ markedly from saw to saw, but disassembly and reassembly will remain pretty much the same for all brands. After all, the basic lower end unit includes the same things, though design factors involving such variables as the number and exact placement of bearings are different. In most cases, the above instructions should get you through a rebuild with any chain saw engine you're likely to run into, assuming the proper torque ratings are available to you.

These two saws were selected because they are typical. Since Homelite and McCulloch dominate the chain saw market in this country, the odds are really excellent that you'll have a saw from one of these companies.

Have a few spare spark plugs on hand when running any newly rebuilt engine. Plug fouling tends to be quite common at this time, so a quick plug change can often eliminate what appears to be a mistake in assembly, and is, actually, only a minor mistake in carburetor tuning.

If the weather is cool, you can start the saw, make all carburetor adjustments, and then let it run through a tank or two of gas (half tank at a time) at fast idle to speed up any needed breakin. Of course, the chain saw should be run either without the chain or in a safe spot. If the temperature is over 50 degrees, *don't* follow the above procedure or the engine may overheat. If the temperature is between freezing and 50°, run through only half a tank of gas at a time, shut down, and allow the saw to cool almost completely before running through the rest of the tank.

OILING SYSTEMS

Chain oiling, by rights, should actually be included in the chapter on chain care, but the fact that the oilers, whether manual or automatic, are located in the powerhead of the saw makes this chapter the most logical place to cover their care and repair. After all, the engine will already be torn down and the oiler exposed if you're doing any sort of a rebuild.

Figures 5-26 and 5-27 illustrate the operation of an automatic chain oiler on a Homelite 150. This oiling system is not supplemented by a manual oiler.

Chain oiler problems are less frequent than would at first seem probable. A rapid check of several things before trying to tear into the oiler can often save time, extra work, and a lot of

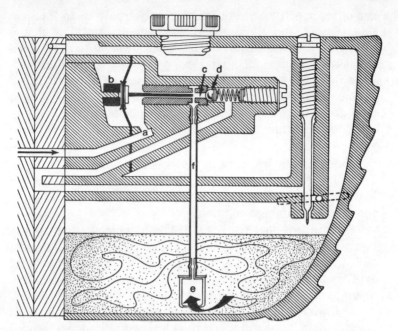

Fig. 5-26. During intake (on downstroke), positive pulse pressure applied to the plunger diaphragm through the pulse channel (a) distends the diaphragm in the direction of the bumper (b), causing low pressure in the pump cavity (c). The check ball (d) remains seated. Oil is drawn through the pickup screen (e) up the rubber tubing (f) into the intake chamber (Courtesy Homelite.)

frustration. First, check the oil tank to make certain it's full. Then move on to the oil holes in the guide bar and on the power head bar mounting pad. If either of these holes are plugged up, nothing is going to move oil to that chain! Look at the guide bar groove. If the chain drive tangs are not sharp enough to clean this groove, oil won't be carried along the bar and chain.

If the tank is full, the oil holes unplugged, and the groove clear, give some thought to the thickness of the chain oil you're using. Oil thickness shouldn't cause any problems at all during warmer months of the year, but when temperatures skid well below freezing, some of those thick chain oils supplied by the chain manufacturers (and some of the saw manufacturers) just will not flow quickly enough to do the job.

Two solutions are possible in such cases: The oil already in the oiler tank can be thinned with kerosene until it flows properly, or you can substitute a lighter weight oil, such as a middleweight motor oil (SAE 20 or 30 depending on the

146

temperature) for cold weather use. Normally, lightweight chain oils won't be needed until outside temperatures skid below 25 degrees. In some heavy-duty cutting situations, the lightweight oils should be used only until the engine, bar, and chain warm up to a good operating temperature. Light oils, especially motor oils, tend to fly off the chain too easily and don't do as good a job of lubrication as you really need.

Should oiler troubles continue, the problem will probably be found in the pump or in the oil tank. The tank should be removed from the powerhead and drained. Then a sealed line and a vacuum tester can be used to check the tank for leaks (Fig. 5-28). If a leak is found, the tank should be replaced. Similar checks should be made on all oil lines, from the pump to the tank and from the tank to the oil discharge holes at the guide bar mounting pad. Since few home mechanics have

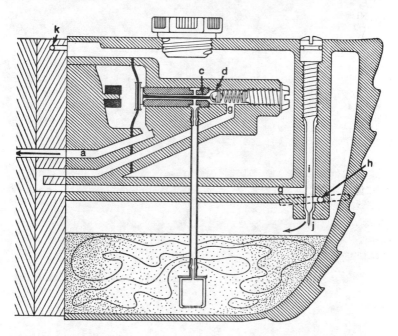

Fig. 5-27. During discharge and bypass (on the upstroke), negative pulse pressure transmitted to the plunger diaphragm distends the diaphragm, driving the plunger to unseat the check ball (d). Oil in the chamber (c) is pumped out through the discharge route (g) and is discharged through hole (h) in the guide bar mounting pad. If the feed rate adjusting valve (i) is opened (counterclockwise), oil will flow through the bypass channel (j) back into the reservoir, thus reducing the rate of flow. There is a tank vent hole at k. (Courtesy Homelite.)

Fig. 5-28. Testing the tank for leaks with a vacuum tester. (Courtesy Homelite.)

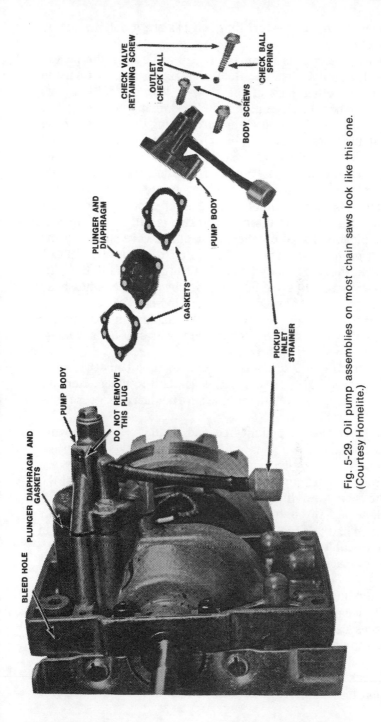

CHECK VALVE RETAINING SCREW

CHECK BALL SPRING

OUTLET CHECK BALL

BODY SCREWS

PLUNGER AND DIAPHRAGM

GASKETS

PUMP BODY

PICKUP INLET STRAINER

BLEED HOLE

PLUNGER DIAPHRAGM AND GASKETS

PUMP BODY

DO NOT REMOVE THIS PLUG

Fig. 5-29. Oil pump assemblies on most chain saws look like this one. (Courtesy Homelite.)

access to a vacuum tester, these checks are usually made by the dealer.

When the tank is removed, it will leave bare the pickup line with its inlet strainer. Before bothering to check out the tank or any other part of the system, look carefully at this strainer. When an oil tank is field filled, many of us forget to wipe off the sawdust and chips surrounding the cap before we open it up. If enough of this debris drops in the tank, the strainer will become clogged. Clean and then recheck the saw for operation (Fig. 5-29). The line from the strainer to the inlet should also be checked. If the rubber is deteriorated, cracked or kinked, the pump cannot operate at full capacity and cannot operate at all if the cracking or kinking is bad enough to shut off the pickup tube altogether. As usual, always check out the simpler problem spots before moving on to the more complex.

When the pump body has been identified and lifted off the engine (most pumps are held in place by a couple of hex head screws), the unit will resemble the one in Fig. 5-29.

First, check the "dry" side of the diaphragm chamber. If there is oil in this side, the diaphragm or its casting is leaking. Determine which it is and replace.

There will be a screw or nut on the pump body that holds the discharge valve spring and check ball in place. Remove the spring and check ball, making sure neither part goes flying across the workbench.

Remove the oil pickup line and strainer, if you haven't already done so.

Now check for obstructions. Among the most likely are dirt, metal chips, and excess silicone sealant used to seal the crankcase to the cylinder.

Blow air through the discharge hole in the guide bar mounting pad and feel for air emerging from the oil passage in the side wall leading into the crankcase.

Spray a low toxicity degreasing solvent all through the passages in the pump body. Homelite recommends Inhibisol. Blow air through the inlet fitting after the degreaser has had time to loosen up dirt and chips. Holes leading from the other passages can alternately be closed with fingertips and then opened to get the greatest air pressure in any one passage at one time.

Check the pump components for condition and correct size relationships. Figure 5-30 shows the desired dimensional

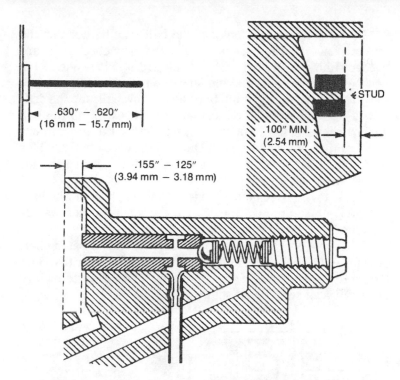

.630" − .620"
(16 mm − 15.7 mm)

.155" − 125"
(3.94 mm − 3.18 mm)

STUD

.100" MIN.
(2.54 mm)

Fig. 5-30. Specifications for pump components. (Courtesy Homelite.)

relationships for the Homelite 150AO. The stud shown must have the proper clearance. That clearance must be as indicated for proper pump operation, or the bumper and stud both will have to be ground down until there is a minimum of 0.100 inch. The plunger must be tight in the collar at the diaphragm end and must slide freely out of and into the pump cylinder. At this point, the plunger must measure from 0.630 to 0.620 inches from its collar to its end.

If the distance from the mounting face of the pump body to the top of the pump cylinder is incorrect, there will be interference with the full stroke at either the intake port or the discharge check ball. Homelite uses a 0.155 to 0.125 inch clearance on the 150AO.

Porosity of the casting or a poor press fit between the cylinder and the casting will cause low output from the pump. This type of problem only shows up when the saw is hot from operation. The only practical repair here is installation of a new pump.

If the check ball is leaking, the ball may be worn or the seat may not fit. The cure is simple. Two new check balls are needed. Remove the old ball and discard it. Place one of the new balls on the seat, making sure the cylinder is supported. Use the correct size drift pin to fit on the new ball; tap the drift with a light hammer (6 ounces or so). This will tap the ball against the seat hard enough to give the seat a new contour and a proper fit on a new ball. Discard the check ball used for reseating and insert the new one. Check the valve spring for distortion, reinstall, and tighten.

Gaskets are used on both sides of the diaphragm when the pump is remounted. On the 150AO, the mounting screws are tightened to 36 inch pounds.

The same checks are performed for a hand operated oiler, with an additional check at the thumb operated lever that does the actual pressurizing for pumping. These systems are generally a lot simpler, as shown in Fig. 5-31.

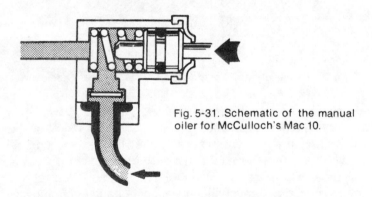

Fig. 5-31. Schematic of the manual oiler for McCulloch's Mac 10.

The following is the disassembly procedure for the manual oiler of a McCulloch Mac 10. To disassemble and service this unit, the oil tank need not be drained, but the fan housing, air filter cover, air filter, carburetor, and the fuel tank must be removed.

Two screws come loose and the housing and gasket (items 2 and 3 in Fig. 5-32) can be lifted off. Take care not to lose the check valve (item 4). Next, pry off the plastic cap (item 5) and take out the plunger and its spring (items 6 and 7). The O ring (item 8) will then slip over the shaft end of the plunger.

Clean all parts with a solvent and make sure they are thoroughly dry. Check all air passages for obstructions and

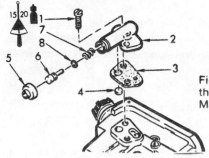

Fig. 5-32. Exploded drawing of the manual oiler on McCulloch's Mac 10.

check the O ring, gasket, and check valve for damage. Replace any damaged parts and clean out any clogged passages.

Check the oiler button and oil rod. If the rod is bent or does not move freely when the button is pressed, then replace.

Reassembly requires coating the new O ring with SAE 30 oil and reversing the disassembly procedure. Make sure the pump mounting pad is clean and use a new gasket. The mounting screws are tightened to 15 to 20 inch pounds and should have a drop of Loctite or Permalock applied before installation (Fig. 5-33).

Check pump operation after completing the assembly.

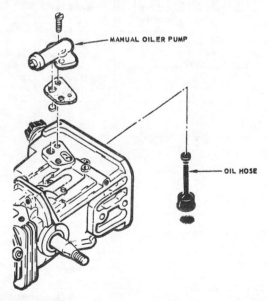

MANUAL OILER PUMP

OIL HOSE

Fig. 5-33. During reassembly of the manual oiler pump, insure that the gasket seals and that the screws are tightened to 15 to 20 inch-pounds. (Courtesy McCulloch.)

MAGNETOS

Fortunately, repairs to the magneto ignition are not needed very often. In general, most ignition problems will occur in the following order: spark plug, breaker points, loose or shorted wiring, improper coil to rotor air gap, condenser, coil, ignition switch, magneto. Spark plug, breaker points, condenser, and the air gap have already been discussed and should be checked first any time ignition problems crop up.

Your next check should be for frayed or loose wiring throughout the ignition system. Occasionally, the rotor may contact the condenser lead and damage it, so make that a first stop on the damaged wiring checklist.

Next comes the testing of other ignition components. The following testing procedures are for the Homelite 150AO, but general disassembly and checking procedures are essentially the same for all saws. Test values for the 150AO are shown in

Table 5-1. Homelite 150AO test values.

	VOM (volt/ohmmeter) 20,000 ohms per volt dc	GRAHAM Model 51 P Model 51 RP	MERC-O-TRONIC Model 98
COIL PRIMARY CONTINUITY	up to 1.6 ohms	2.7 ohms max. impedance	1.6 ohms (same as VOM)
SECONDARY CONTINUITY		9300 ohms max. resistance	
MAXIMUM SECONDARY			Scale Reading 55-65
COIL INDEX		75 max. (scale setting)	
COIL FIRING TEST (MINIMUM GAP TEST)		min. of 30 at 75 coil index.	good steady spark at 2.2 amperes, max.
GAP INDEX		62 max.	
CONDENSER CAPACITY		.15-.19 mfd	.15-.19 mfd
CONDENSER SERIES RESISTANCE		1 ohm	green block scale (not red section)
CAPACITOR LEAKAGE (insulation leakage test)		Min. 20 megohms at room temp.	needle deflection and return to zero according to tester instructions.

Table 5-1. You can get ignition test specifications for your particular saw from your dealer.

Primary Circuit Test With VOM or Test Light

Hookup: Disconnect coil ground lead from the core. Connect one lead of tester to the insulated side of the switch terminal on the top rib of the cylinder. Connect other lead to the coil ground lead (or to any common engine ground).

Test: For VOM resistance check, set meter for R × 1 (R times 1) and read the R × 1 scale up to the maximum of 1.6 ohms. For continuity check with a test light; rock the rotor back and forth so the magnets pass by the core legs and points open and close. The test light should go on and off, a rough indication of make-and-break circuitry (Fig. 5-34).

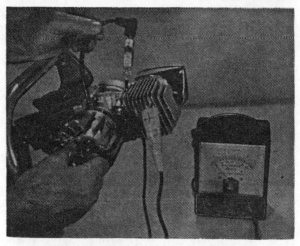

Fig. 5-34. Testing with a VOM. (Courtesy Homelite).

Coil Test Series With a Merc-o-tronic Ignition Analyzer Model 98

The Merc-o-tronic Ignition Analyzer Model 98 is shown in Fig. 5-35. Remember, *do not* plug into power line during coil testing. Always make tests in the following sequence.

Test 1 for Coil Power and Test 2 for High-Speed Power:

1. Pry off the breaker box cover with two screwdrivers. Put a piece of cardboard between the breaker points to insulate them.

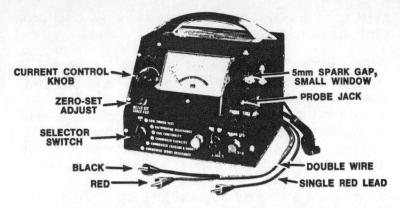

CURRENT CONTROL KNOB

ZERO-SET ADJUST

SELECTOR SWITCH

BLACK

RED

5mm SPARK GAP, SMALL WINDOW

PROBE JACK

DOUBLE WIRE

SINGLE RED LEAD

Fig. 5-35. The Merc-o-tronic Ignition Analyzer Model 98.

2. Connect black test lead to the coil primary ground wire, and the small red test lead to the coil primary lead (if disconnected) or to the insulated side of the switch terminal (Fig. 5-36).

3. Connect single red test lead to the terminal of the spark plug wire.

4. When hookup has been made, turn the current control knob to the extreme left. Turn selector switch to "POSITION 1, COIL POWER TEST". Slowly turn current control knob clockwise; observe scale 1 and watch for spark to occur across the 5mm electrode gap in the small window:

    a) The maximum amperage before which a strong, steady spark should occur is 2.2 on scale 1.

    b) A strong coil will begin to spark at about 1.1 amperes, spark steadily above 1.2 amperes, and the dial turn to the maximum before the needle reaches 2.2 amperes.

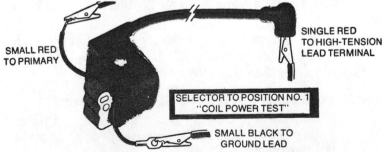

SMALL RED TO PRIMARY

SINGLE RED TO HIGH-TENSION LEAD TERMINAL

SELECTOR TO POSITION NO. 1 "COIL POWER TEST"

SMALL BLACK TO GROUND LEAD

Fig. 5-36. Test 1 for coil power (Courtesy Homelite.)

c) A maximum reading (of 2.2 amperes or more before steady spark) introduces the possibility that the coil performance is marginal.

d) No spark, weak spark, or intermittent spark by 2.2 amperes indicates a faulty coil.

5. Continue to turn the current control knob clockwise after steady spark occurs. If you can turn it all the way to the right and get steady spark, the coil output is good under simulated high-speed firing conditions.

Test 3—Probing for Coil Surface Insulation Leaks:

Warning: This test puts a severe strain on the coil, so it should be completed as rapidly as possible and the analyzer turned off. Do not let the probe linger at any point—play it lightly along the insulated surfaces of the high-tension lead and the coil.

1. Leave the small red and black test leads connected as in tests 1 and 2, but remove the single red test lead from the high-tension lead terminal.

2. Plug the test probe into the test probe jack on front panel of tester. Turn selector switch to position 1. Turn current control knob to HI position for maximum current reading on the meter.

Note: Do not exceed the meter maximum reading of 2.2 amperes for this coil.

a) If there is no spark there is no leak.

b) A faint spark or glow occurring around the coil during probing is a corona which does not indicate a defect.

c) At a leak, sparks will jump to the probe.

Test 4 for Coil Continuity (Tests Primary and Secondary):

1. Turn selector switch to "#3 COIL CONTINUITY" and clip the small red and black test leads together. Turn meter adjustment knob for scale 3 until the pointer lines up on the "SET" position on right end of scale 3.

2. Connect small black test lead coil ground wire, and small red test lead to high-tension lead terminal (Fig. 5-37).

3. The reading obtained should be between 7500 and 9300 ohms. An excellent coil usually gives a reading of about 8300 ohms during this test.

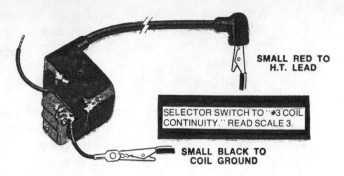

SMALL RED TO
H.T. LEAD

SELECTOR SWITCH TO "#3 COIL
CONTINUITY." READ SCALE 3.

SMALL BLACK TO
COIL GROUND

Fig. 5-37. Test 4 for coil continuity (tests primary and secondary). (Courtesy Homelite.)

Test 5 for Coil Primary Resistance:

1. Do not clip test leads together. Turn selector switch to "# 2 DISTRIBUTOR RESISTANCE" for checking low *ohm* resistance values.
2. Turn meter adjustment knob. Line up the pointer on the set position on right end of scale #2. This sets meter for low ohm values from 0 to 30 ohms.
3. Clip small red test lead to primary lead after disconnecting the lead from the junction block. Connect small black test lead to ground lead after disconnecting lead from coil core (Fig. 5-38).
4. Read the *red* figures on scale 2: The dc resistance of the windings should be the same as for the test with a VOM—up to 1.6 ohms.
   a) If considerably lower than 1.6 ohms, there is a short between some of the windings in the

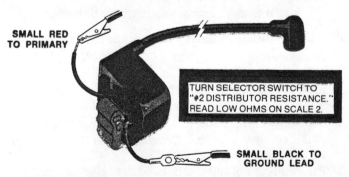

SMALL RED
TO PRIMARY

TURN SELECTOR SWITCH TO
"#2 DISTRIBUTOR RESISTANCE."
READ LOW OHMS ON SCALE 2.

SMALL BLACK TO
GROUND LEAD

Fig. 5-38. Test 5 for coil primary resistance. Do not clip test leads together. (Courtesy Homelite.)

primary. A 10% short will lower the secondary output by as much as 1500 volts.

b) Readings above 1.6 ohms indicate an open condition in the coil.

Test 6 for Grounded Coil:

1. Leave small black lead connected to coil ground wire as in test 5. Connect small red test lead to common ground (to unit) (Fig. 5-39).

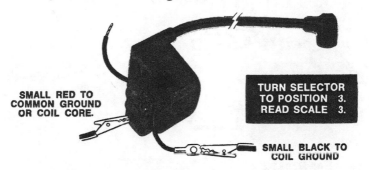

SMALL RED TO COMMON GROUND OR COIL CORE.

TURN SELECTOR TO POSITION 3. READ SCALE 3.

SMALL BLACK TO COIL GROUND

Fig. 5-39. Test 6 for grounded coil. (Courtesy Homelite.)

2. Turn selector switch to position 3 and read scale 3.
   a) The pointer hand must be on the "ZERO" line at left end of scale 3.
   b) Any pointer movement (except for momentary deflection as selector knob is turned to position 3 indicates a ground.
3. If there is a needle deflection in step 2, disconnect the breaker arm spring from the terminal, and disconnect the primary coil wire from the junction block. If the meter pointer remains to the right, this part of the magneto is probably O.K. Check the condenser for a short and the breaker points for improper (grounded) assembly.

Condenser Tests With the Merc-o-tronic Ignition Analyzer

The Merc-o-tronic Ignition Analyzer Model 98 is shown in Fig. 5-35.

Test 1 for Capacity (Plug Into 115 Volt-60 Cycle Outlet):

1. Remove condenser from the unit, plug analyzer into 115 volt-60 cycle outlet, and place selector switch on position "#4 CONDENSER CAPACITY."

2. Clip small red and black test leads together, depress red button, and turn meter adjustment knob to line up pointer at set line on right end of scale 4. Unclip the test leads.
3. Connect small red test lead to condenser lead and small black to condenser mounting clamp (Fig. 5-40).
4. Depress red button to obtain reading on scale 4. The reading must be within 15 and 19 mfd (microfarads) on scale 4.

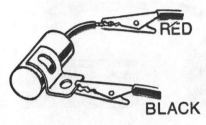

RED

BLACK

Fig. 5-40. Test 1 for capacity. (Courtesy Homelite.)

Test 2 For Leakage:
1. Leave everything as it was at completion of test 1 *except* turn the selector switch to position "#5 LEAKAGE AND SHORT."
2. Depress and hold red button for at least 15 seconds; read scale 5:
    a) The pointer will deflect to the right, but must return to within the range of the black bar at the left end of scale 5.
    b) Any readings to the right of the black bar indicate either a leaking or shorted condenser.

Test 3 For Series Resistance:
1. Disconnect leads from condenser, and turn selector switch to position "#6 CONDENSER SERIES RESISTANCE." Plug into a 115 volt, 60 cycle outlet.
2. Clip small red and black test leads together and adjust meter "set scale #6" to set line 2 on right end of scale 6.
3. Reconnect small red test lead to condenser lead, and small black lead to condenser mounting clamp.
4. Meter pointer must be within the green block at right end of scale 6 or slightly more to the right, *but not to the left*.

5. While testing, move and wiggle the condenser lead; any pointer movement may indicate a loose connection between condenser and lead.

Coil Test Series With the Graham Coil Condenser Tester Model 51P or 51RP

This tester plugs into a 115 volt, 60 cycle outlet and requires a warm up period with test selector knob set to "COIL STAND-BY."

Test 1 for Primary Continuity:
1. Hookup:
   a) Disconnect ground lead from coil core to isolate the coil secondary during testing. Connect one lead of tester to insulated side of the ignition switch terminal. Connect other lead to any common engine ground.
   b) To test "off the unit," connect one lead coil primary wire and the other to coil ground wire. *Do not test on a metal bench.*
2. Turn indicator dial to "PRIMARY CONTINUITY."
3. For test a) "on the unit:" rock the rotor back and forth so the points open and close and the magnets pass by the core legs. The meter needle should deflect left and right from 0 to 100 as the points open and close, indicating that the breaker points are opening and closing.
4. For test b) "off the unit:" the meter should read 2.7 ohms impedance. Note that the impedance or "ac ohms" is different from the resistance readings (dc ohms) which would be obtained with a VOM type of tester.

Test 2 For Secondary Continuity:
1. Hookup: With the coil off the unit and coil ground lead disconnected, attach test clips to the end of the high-tension lead and to the coil ground lead.
2. Put selector knob (middle dial) to "SECONDARY CONTINUITY."
3. Then maximum reading should be 9300 ohms, but can be 20 percent lower.

161

Test 3 (This is a three-part test sequence):

Caution: Do not let anyone touch the coil during any of the following tests without first putting center dial pointer to "0-20V coil index."

1. For this series of tests, it is important to set the firing power of the primary to that necessary to generate the required Secondary Open Voltage required for valid testing. This happens to be 75 on the dial and is merely a reference number.

Caution: The coil index of 75 should never be exceeded while the coil is connected to the tester. Do not test on a metal bench.

2. Hook up for coil index: Connect one test lead to the ground wire and the other test lead to the coil primary lead.

3. Procedure: Point selector knob to "0-20 V COIL INDEX." Turn "COIL INDEX" pointer to the "DECREASE" end of the dial. Hold "COIL TESTS" knob in the "ON" position and slowly turn the "COIL INDEX" knob toward "INCREASE" until needle points to 75 on the top line of the tester.

4. Coil firing test (of coil's ability to fire at minimum energization): This test is also known as "MINIMUM COIL TEST." After setting to coil index of 75 turn selector knob from "0-20 V COIL INDEX" to "STAND-BY COIL TEST." *Do not touch coil!* Turn "COIL TESTS" knob to "ON" and hold it there. The needle should deflect and hold steady. A reading of 30 is the specified minimum but an excellent coil may test as high as 38.

Warning: Let go of "COIL TESTS" knob and return selector knob to "0-20 V COIL INDEX" before touching coil or going on to the next phase of this test.

Chapter 6
Electric Chain Saws

Electric Chain Saws

The electric chain saw user has a few things going in his favor: no tuneups ever needed, a lot less noise, no exhaust fumes, and, in general, much simpler repair needs during the life of the chain saw. Since when are electrical repairs easier than internal combustion engine repairs? Well, since these chain saws have been made so that individual parts replacement or repair is seldom, if ever, needed.

Clutch replacement is possible and desirable when the clutch unit becomes worn. The replacement is carried out very much as it is on a gasoline driven chain saw, so the basic instruction provided back in Chapter 5 will serve very well.

One of the major difficulties with any electric saw, whether a chain saw, circular saw, or saber saw, is the certainty that sooner or later the user is going to cut through the power cord. The replacement of this cord, though, is very simple. A quick look at Fig. 6-1 will show how most cords attach to the saws. Of course, the saw must be unplugged and care taken when attaching the new cord to the terminals. Make sure the terminal screws are snugged down tight.

Oil pumping on electric chain saws is very much like that on gasoline driven chain saws, so the tests for those pumps can be carried out with any electric saw.

As Fig. 6-1 and Fig. 6-2 show, electric chain saws are fairly easy to disassemble. To disassemble the Skil saw in Fig. 6-2, first remove the chain and guide bar. Next, the cases are pulled apart by removing the appropriate screws, nuts, and bolts.

A gear puller should be used to remove gear number 3 (Fig. 6-2) after the clutch is removed. The inner casing can then be removed, giving access to the fan on the end of the armature. This fan should be checked for clogging and damaged blades. Generally it will be just fine since it is very well protected inside the housing.

Moving to the other side of the saw, the screws holding the motor in the case can be removed and the motor lifted out.

From this point, the motor comes apart into two major components: the armature and the field. Special equipment is needed to test the field and armature windings, so these parts will have to be brought to a dealer for testing (make sure he has a shop because many of these saws are sold through stores that do little or none of their own repair work).

A thorough check of all wiring will help to prevent any future problems. The field terminal, for instance, can wear and fray a bit under heavy use, so making sure that it has maintained contact can often return an inoperative saw to use without requiring that the field be replaced.

Of course, brushes eventually wear out on all electric motors. They must be regularly checked and replaced when too worn to keep the saw operating well. Fortunately, modern chain saws, such as the Skil and Roper, provide easy access to their brushes. So, in most cases, no major disassembly of the saw is needed. Simply remove the screws or holders covering the brushes, and the brush springs, and then remove and check the brushes (31, 32, and 33, Fig. 6-2). Replace as needed.

An ohmmeter can be used to check for continuity in the switch should the chain saw ever completely refuse to operate. Make sure the saw is unplugged whenever an ohmmeter is used or you'll burn out the meter.

If the meter indicates an open when the switch is on, then the switch needs to be replaced.

Other than replacing a cut power cord every so often, that's about all you'll need to do with an electric chain saw. Proper lubrication will, naturally, help to add years to the life of the chain saw.

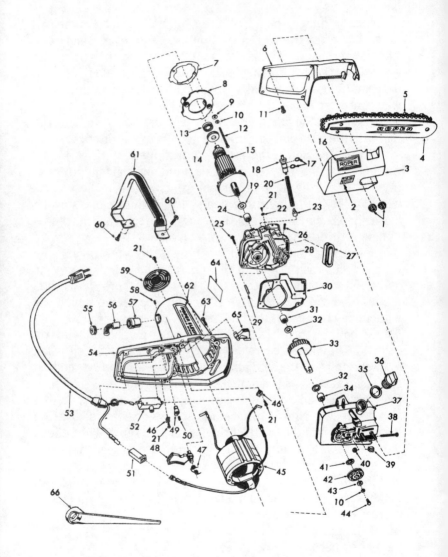

KEY NO.	DESCRIPTION	KEY NO.	DESCRIPTION
1	Guide Bar Nut	33	Gear and Shaft Assembly
2	Decal	34	Needle Bearing
3	Chain Shield	35	"O" Ring
4	Guide Bar	36	Oil Tank Cap
5	Chain	37	Gear Case Bar Support Assembly (Inc. Key No's. 34 and 41)
6	Handle Cover		
7	Air Gasket		
8	Air Baffle	38	Slotted Pan Hd. Machine Screw No. 10-24 UNC x 2 Lg. Heat Treated
9	Flat Washer 7/32 x ½ x 18 Ga.		
10	Lockwasher No. 10		
11	Slotted Fil. Hd. Machine Screw-Self Tap Type 23, No. 10-24 UNC x ½ Lg.	39	Chain Tightener Block
		40	Huglock Nut
		41	Oil Seal
12	Slotted Pan Hd. Machine Screw-Self Tap Type 23, No. 10-24 UNC x 3 Lg.	42	Sprocket
		43	Sprocket Retainer
		44	Hex Hd. Screw No. 10-24 UNC x 3/8 Lg. Heat Treated
13	Ball Bearing		
14	Fibre Washer		
15	Rotor and Bearing Assembly (Inc. Key No's. 13 and 14)	45	Field
		46	Wire Clip
16	Decal	47	Throttle Spring
17	"O" Ring	48	Throttle Lever
18	Oil Pump	49	Throttle Lock
19	Fibre Washer	50	Detent Spring
20	Oil Pickup Hose	51	Terminal Housing
21	Slotted Pan Hd. Machine Screw-Self Tap Type 23, No. 6-32 UNC x 5/16	52	Switch
		53	Cord Set
		54	Motor Housing
22	Flat Washer 5/32 x 3/8 x 20 Ga.	55	Brush Holder Cap
23	Oil Filter	56	Brush, Cap and Spring
24	Needle Bearing	57	Brush Holder
25	Slotted Fil. Hd. Machine Screw-Self Tap Type 1, No. 8-32 UNC x 7/8 lg.	58	Hex Socket Headless Set Screw-Cup Point No. 10-24 UNC x ¼ Lg.
26	Cotter Pin 1/16 x 3/8		
27	Sight Gage	59	Air Screen
28	Gear Case Assembly (Inc. No's. 17, 18, 20, 21, 22, 23, 24, 26, 27, 29 and 31)	60	Pan Hd. Slotted Thread Self Tap Screw Type 23, No. 10-24 UNC x ¾ Lg.
		61	Front Handle
29	Roll Pin	62	Decal
30	Gasket	63	Slotted Fil. Hd. Machine Screw No. 10-24 UNC x ½ Lg.
31	Needle Bearing		
32	Fibre Washer	64	Model Number Plate
		65	Oil Pump Lever
		66	Wrench
		----	Owners Manual

Fig. 6-1. A Roper electric chain saw, model C-00032RO.

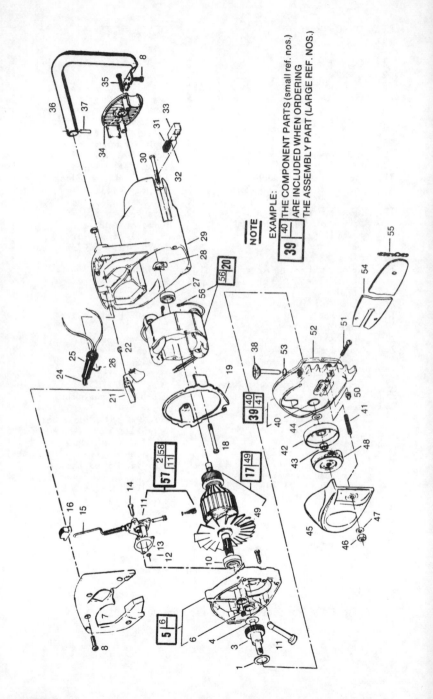

NOTE

EXAMPLE:

| 39 | 40 | THE COMPONENT PARTS (small ref. nos.) ARE INCLUDED WHEN ORDERING THE ASSEMBLY PART (LARGE REF. NOS.) |

168

REF. NO.	PART NAME
1	WASHER...AS REQ.
2	OIL FILTER
3	GEAR SPINDLE
4	WASHER
5	BEARING PLATE ASSEMBLY
6	BEARING
7	HANDLE COVER
8	SCREW
9	SCREW
10	BALL BEARING
11	OIL PUMP
12	"O"RING
13	PUMP GASKET
14	SCREW
15	PUMP ROD
16	OILER BUTTON
17	ARMATURE (115 V.)
18	SCREW
19	BAFFLE
20	FIELD (115 V.)
21	SWITCH...1
22	WASHER...1
23	SAFETY SWITCH BUTTON
24	CORD & CAP
25	CORD GUARD
26	CORD CLAMP
27	BALL BEARING
28	SPRING LOADING WASHER
29	MOTOR HOUSING
30	SCREW
31	BRUSH
32	BRUSH SPRING
33	BRUSH HOLDER
34	END COVER
35	SCREW
36	HANDLE
37	HANDLE PIN
38	OIL LEVEL INDICATOR
39	GEAR HOUSING ASSEMBLY
40	BEARING
41	STUD...1
42	SPROCKET & DRUM
43	BEARING
44	WASHER
45	CLUTCH COVER
46	NUT
47	FLAT WASHER
48	CLUTCH
49	FAN
50	BAR ADJUSTER NUT
51	SCREW
52	GASKET
53	GASKET
54	GUIDE BAR
55	CHAIN
56	TERMINAL
57	OIL PUMP & FILTER ASSEM.
58	TUBING

Fig. 6-2. A Skil model 1602 type 1 electric chain saw.

169

Chapter 7
Chain Care

Chain Care

Installing a new saw chain is one of the more frequent replacement jobs on any chain saw. First, make certain the ignition switch is off. Then remove the nuts holding the drive case on and lift the cover off the guide bar mounting pad.

There will be a mounting plate on the guide bar and this outer plate must be removed. It just slips off over the bolts. Now, slide off the guide bar and lift the old chain off the sprocket, leaving the inner mounting plate in place. Gloves or rags should be used to protect the fingers and hands while working with any saw chain.

As shown in Fig. 7-1, line up the guide bar with the mounting bolts and place it up against the inner mounting plate, after making sure the oil discharge holes in the mounting pad and on the guide bar are clean.

Line up the new chain with the teeth facing in the direction of rotation, as shown in Fig. 7-2. The direction of rotation will have the teeth along the upper portion of the guide bar facing *away* from the sprocket.

The chain will have to be looped and angled to fit through the small space between the drive case and the clutch so that it then fits over the drive sprocket. Make sure you don't kink the chain as you are slipping it in place or you'll have to remove it and get the knots out (Fig. 7-3).

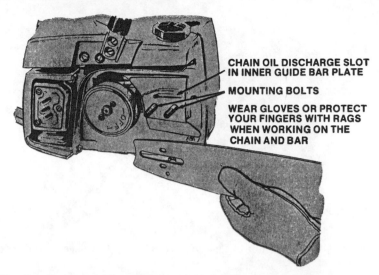

CHAIN OIL DISCHARGE SLOT
IN INNER GUIDE BAR PLATE

MOUNTING BOLTS

WEAR GLOVES OR PROTECT
YOUR FINGERS WITH RAGS
WHEN WORKING ON THE
CHAIN AND BAR

Fig. 7-1. To remount the guide bar, first slide the mounting bolts through the slot in the guide bar. (Courtesy Homelite.)

Starting at the top of the drive sprocket, feed the chain drive links into the top bar groove, as shown in Fig. 7-4. This process will continue right on around the nose of the guide bar.

Now pull the bar out in the direction of the bar nose to remove the slack from the chain. If any drive links pop out of the bar groove, slip them back into the groove before continuing.

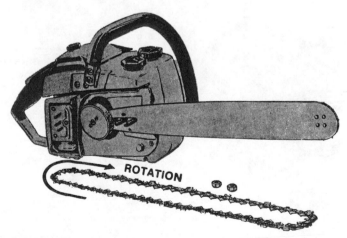

ROTATION

Fig. 7-2. Make sure the teeth are facing in the direction of rotation. (Courtesy Homelite.)

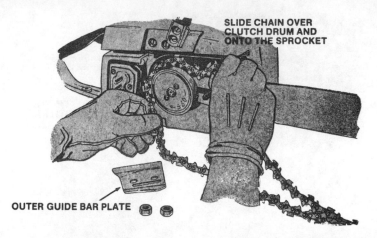

Fig. 7-3. Be careful not to kink the chain during installation. (Courtesy Homelite.)

There will be a chain tension adjusting screw on the engine case, either to the inside of the guide bar and close to its bottom or on the outside of the case near the mounting bolts for the guide bar. Turn this screw until it appears certain that the adjustor pin will engage the hole in the guide bar when the cover is fitted in place (Fig. 7-5).

Now slide the cover into place, keeping a check on the pin as the cover goes in place. Put the chain guard nuts back on

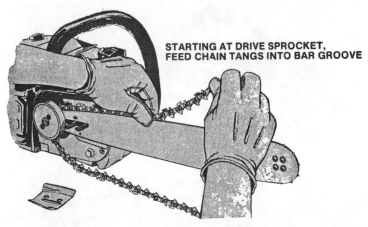

Fig. 7-4. Begin at the top of the drive sprocket and place the chain drive links in the bar groove, working your way clockwise around the guide bar. (Courtesy Homelite.)

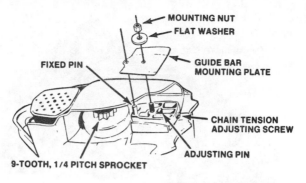

MOUNTING NUT
FLAT WASHER
GUIDE BAR MOUNTING PLATE
FIXED PIN
CHAIN TENSION ADJUSTING SCREW
ADJUSTING PIN
9-TOOTH, 1/4 PITCH SPROCKET

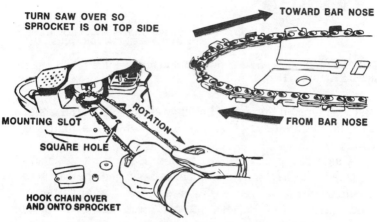

TURN SAW OVER SO SPROCKET IS ON TOP SIDE

TOWARD BAR NOSE

ROTATION

FROM BAR NOSE

MOUNTING SLOT

SQUARE HOLE

HOOK CHAIN OVER AND ONTO SPROCKET

Fig. 7-5. The adjusting pin must engage the hole in the guide bar. Turn the chain tension adjusting screw to insure proper engagement. (Courtesy Homelite.)

the bolts (or the bolt back into its hole on some saws) and run them up finger tight temporarily (Fig. 7-6). Check the assembly. Make sure the chain slides freely over the guide bar

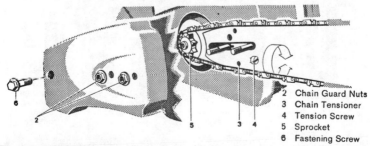

2 Chain Guard Nuts
3 Chain Tensioner
4 Tension Screw
5 Sprocket
6 Fastening Screw

Fig. 7-6. After the guide bar is in place, replace the chain guard nuts on the bolts. (Courtesy Solo.)

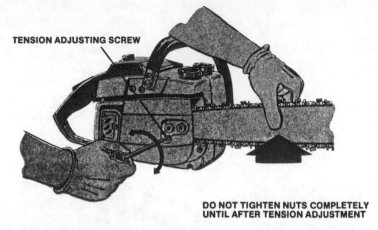

DO NOT TIGHTEN NUTS COMPLETELY
UNTIL AFTER TENSION ADJUSTMENT

Fig. 7-7. Hold the guide bar upward during the entire tensioning procedure. (Courtesy Homelite.)

and then tension the chain, holding the nose up all the while, as covered in Chapter 3 (Fig. 7-7). Then tighten the chain guard nuts.

Guide bar problems are varied. Each time the chain is replaced, the bar should be checked out and the bar groove should be cleaned. Figure 7-8 shows common wear patterns for guide bar grooves. Pattern number 2 is a fault that can often be corrected by a dealer with a machine shop. Burred guide rails (pattern number 3) should be filed to remove the burrs. Pattern number 4 shows a set of rails worn badly from a too loose saw chain. The only cure here is replacement of the guide rail. Spread rails (pattern number 5) can often be tapped closed with a soft faced hammer. Any tapping should be done gently and checked often to make certain the rails aren't

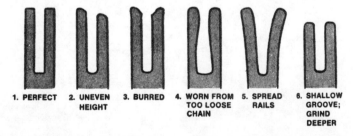

1. PERFECT   2. UNEVEN   3. BURRED   4. WORN FROM   5. SPREAD   6. SHALLOW
                  HEIGHT   TOO LOOSE   RAILS   GROOVE;
                                            CHAIN   GRIND
                                                                         DEEPER

Fig. 7-8. Wear patterns of guide bar grooves and bar rails. (Courtesy Homelite.)

closed down too much. Spread rails tapped too far in can be respread with a gentle prying from the tip of a screwdriver. The key word for any work on guide rails is *gently*. Do it easy and it will work, whether the rails are being closed up, spread, or filed. A too shallow guide rail groove (pattern number 6) can sometimes be reground at the dealer shop.

Saw chain filing is a simple job, one that requires time and care if done freehand, and one that can be quickly done with one or two simple tools. A File-n-Joint is one of the best tools for working on a saw chain; it cuts the time of chain sharpening by better than 50 percent. If a File-n-Joint is not used, a file holder should be, because holding the correct filing angle for a series of teeth can be very difficult if done freehand. Most chain saw teeth are filed at 35 degrees.

There are two ways to determine if a chain needs sharpening. First, if the wood debris you are getting from the chain is mostly *dust*, then the chain is dull. The debris should contain fairly large chips (Fig. 7-9). Second, the chain can be checked simply by examining the cutting edges. As shown in Fig. 7-10, the cutting edges of a sharp chain do not reflect light, while those of a dull chain do.

Fig. 7-9. A sharp chain saw leaves wood debris that looks like this.

Fig. 7-10. Sharp cutting edges do not reflect light; dull cutting edges do.
(Courtesy Homelite.)

When the chain needs sharpening, and you want to do the job on the guide bar, simply tighten the chain so that it doesn't wobble on the bar. Insert the correct size chain file in the file holder (or clamp the File-n-Joint to the guide bar as shown in its instructions) (Fig. 7-11). Place the file against the cutter face at the correct angle. Make sure the file stays level with no dipping or rocking movement. File the teeth, in one direction only—towards the front corner of the teeth. Move the file away from the face of the tooth on the return stroke. Use a light, firm pressure, with the pressure being applied towards the back of the tooth. Downward pressure should be avoided. A file holder will keep ten percent of the file above the top plate of the chain and this will automatically produce a beveled and hollow-ground underedge on the tooth.

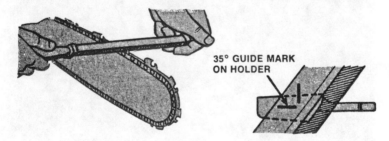

35° GUIDE MARK
ON HOLDER

Fig. 7-11. Cutters must be sharpened at the proper angles. (Courtesy Homelite.)

Each tooth should have only a few firm strokes for normal sharpening. Generally, three to four should be plenty. All cutters on one side of the chain should be filed first, then the cutters on the other side. Figure 7-12 shows the correct filing angles for most chains.

If the file is rotated in the file holder once in a while, a clean file edge will be used for most of the cutting and a better job will result.

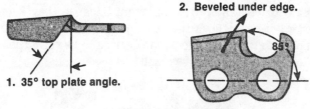

2. Beveled under edge.

1. 35° top plate angle.

3. Side plate 85° to line of chain travel.

Fig. 7-12. Most chain saw cutters should be filed to these angles. (Courtesy Homelite.)

It is essential that all cutter teeth be filed to the same length or inefficient cutting will result (Fig. 7-13). Each tooth, to do its share of the cutting job, must be no longer, and no shorter, than its fellows.

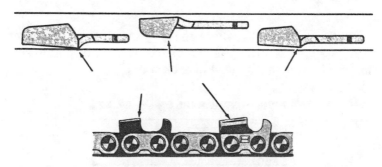

Fig. 7-13. If some cutters are longer than others, file them back to the length of the short cutters. (Courtesy Homelite.)

Also, teeth must be filed back past damaged areas: if one tooth is so filed, all others must then be brought down to the same size (Fig. 7-14). If the chain is chromed, then the filing must go past the point of damage or wear to the chrome on the teeth.

Fig. 7-14. File cutters back past damaged areas. (Courtesy Homelite.)

Chain drive tangs are important because they keep the guide bar groove clear of sawdust. As shown in Fig. 7-15, every fourth or fifth tang will occasionally need to be resharpened in order to keep the bar groove clear.

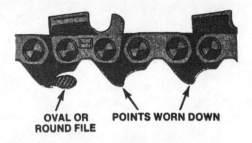

OVAL OR ROUND FILE   POINTS WORN DOWN

Fig. 7-15. Chain drive tangs also need to be sharpened occasionally. (Courtesy Homelite.)

Figure 7-16 shows where the forward edge of the cutter must line up when filing is completed. It must be on the kerf line of the saw chain and not in back of it.

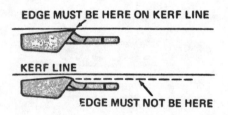

EDGE MUST BE HERE ON KERF LINE

KERF LINE

EDGE MUST NOT BE HERE

Fig. 7-16. The forward edges of cutters must line up properly. (Courtesy Homelite.)

Tooth faults requiring extensive refiling are shown in Table 7-1. The table includes a discussion of the problems and the causes.

Depth gauge clearance is important. Every second or third time the teeth are sharpened, or if a large amount of steel is removed from the cutters, the depth gauges should be jointed to correct depth. If the gauges are too high, the chain teeth will not get a good bite; if too low, the teeth will take too large a bite, causing the chain to grab and jerk. If some gauges are higher than others, the chain will cut off line, favoring the side having the lowest gauges.

Table 7-1. Tooth faults and causes. (Courtesy Homelite.)

Fault	Cause
FORWARD HOOK Chain will grab and jerk producing rough cutting.	Caused by excessive downward filing pressure, or tip of file held too low on tooth.
BACK SLOPE Chain resists entering wood (scrapes instead of cutting wood). Causes excessive heat and wear to bar and chain.	Caused by lowering handle end of file, or holding file too high on the tooth.
IMPROPER TOP PLATE ANGLES Blunt chain requires too much feed pressure. This top plate angle causes chain to bind, produces a rough cut, robs power from saw, and increases bar groove wear.	Caused by holding file at wrong angle, or letting it drift or rock during the stroke.
CUTTERS FILED AT NONMATCHING ANGLES Chain will not cut at its best. May cut off line or "run" to one side; drag may slow down motor.	Caused by letting pressure and filing angle vary from tooth to tooth, or one side filed with different angles and lengths than the other.
THIN FEATHERED EDGES When they almost immediately break off, you have a dull chain. Usually found on chain filed with a hook (see "forward hook").	Caused by holding file with handle too low, or pressing back or down too hard on file
BLUNT CUTTING EDGES Although edge is durable it won't cut properly; scrapes wood, robs power, and produces dust instead of chips.	Caused by holding file too high on face of tooth, or keeping file handle too high.

Use a depth gauge jointer and a safe-edge (no teeth on edge) flat file. Fit the jointer over the chain so that the slotted end of the jointer points toward the bar nose and the depth gauge projects up through the slot (Fig. 7-17). File the depth gauge flush with the top of the jointer. File all gauges to this height.

Fig. 7-17. Depth gauges should be filed to the proper depth. (Courtesy Homelite.)

A worn drive sprocket can cause a number of problems. Figure 7-18 shows two types of drive sprockets with their wear patterns. These sprockets are relatively inexpensive and should be replaced whenever wear starts to show. Any saw used with a sprocket nose bar should have the drive sprocket replaced whenever the sprocket nose is replaced. In fact, the best results will be had by replacing both sprockets and the chain all at the same time.

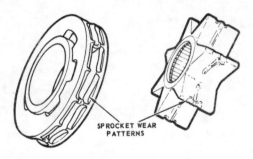

SPROCKET WEAR
PATTERNS

Fig. 7-18. Two different kinds of drive sprockets and their wear patterns. (Courtesy McCulloch.)

Replacing a worn sprocket nose is a fairly simple job. The following replacement procedure generally applies to most chain saws. The number of rivets and the shape of the nose may vary from brand to brand.

1. Drill through the centers of the three rivets shown in Fig. 7-19 (do not remove the other rivets) and punch them out of the holes.

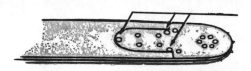

Fig. 7-19. Punch out only the rivets indicated by the arrows when removing the sprocket nose from the bar. (Courtesy Homelite.)

2. Clamp the bar nose right over the rivet heads in a vise and strike the end of the guide bar mounting slot with a rod and hammer to free up and remove the nose (Fig. 7-20).

Fig. 7-20. Lock the nose in a vise and use a rod and hammer to knock the bar loose from the nose. (Courtesy Homelite.)

3. Slide the replacement nose into place until the rivet holes in bar and nose line up.
4. Insert the three rivets and place bar on a supporting surface. Peen the rivet heads smoothly with light taps of the ball head of the hammer, then strike several blows with the flat head of the hammer until rivets fill up the holes (Fig. 7-21).

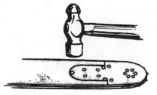

Fig. 7-21. Peen the rivets lightly to correct the round shape, then flatten the heads so the rivets fill up the holes. (Courtesy Homelite.)

5. Assemble bar and chain on the saw, preoil the chain with the manual oiler, and run-in for one minute or more at slow speed without cutting. Making a few light boring cuts with the nose will also help set the proper wear pattern for the nose sprocket and bearing. Be careful of kickback during boring.

Chapter 8
Accessories

Accessories

There are lots of things that can make working with a chain saw easier. Fortunately, most of these things are relatively inexpensive.

Some chain saws offer a series of toothed bumpers, known as bumper spikes, that are handy in log bucking. If your chain saw is equipped to use bumper spikes, they may well be included in the package you buy. If they're not included, check to see if there are two threaded holes at the base of the guide bar. If there are, your dealer can find out whether or not bumper spikes are available to fit your particular saw. For the top of the line chain saws, you'll even have a length selection, medium and long. Go with the medium length for speed of movement.

When bucking a log, the spike is jammed against the log just as the chain starts to cut. As long as the log is smaller around than the saw's guide bar is long, the saw can be pivoted into the cut using the spikes as a base, allowing a bit more relaxation of the arm and shoulder muscles during extensive cutting. Installation is simple for all models (Fig. 8-1). For heavy-duty bucking of logs smaller around than the guide bar length, the bumper spikes can be a big energy saver.

The bow saw guide is another accessory. The bow saw guide is nothing more than a heavy duty loop of metal that replaces the guide bar. A specially sized chain is also needed,

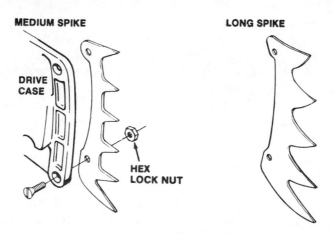

Fig. 8-1. A medium bumper spike and a long bumper spike. (Courtesy Homelite.)

and, in many cases, a couple of holes will have to be drilled in the drive case cover of the engine. In a few other cases, some metal must also be ground off this case cover for correct fitting of the bow guide. The maker of the bow guide unit or the chain saw will provide templates and directions if the saw is designed to be used with bow saw guides.

One expert states flatly that the bow saw attachment is of little use to any person not suffering from terminal laziness. Basically the bow saw attachment enables you to cut a tree with a single, angled cut made from the back side of the tree. Usually, the cut will be made with the saw tip angled down to the base of the tree. Bow saw guides are usually suitable only for cutting down trees up to 10 inches in diameter, but when many trees of that size have to come down, the operator can save a lot of time and energy using the bow saw guide.

Bow saws can also prove handy for bucking smaller logs when there is a chance of a solid guide bar getting pinched and hung up.

The nuts attaching the bow saw guide to the chain saw powerhead must be torqued, usually to 70 or more inch-pounds. The bow saw chain is installed in much the same manner as is any saw chain, with the same precautions about wearing gloves, removing kinks from the chain, and so on. The chain is then tensioned in the same manner as for any other solid nose guide bar.

Wedges can be good things to have around when using chain saws. Remember that any wedge likely to come in contact with the moving chain should be made of a material considerably softer than the chain. Good bucking and felling wedges will be made of no harder material than aluminum, with many made of hard plastic and wood. There's no reason on earth you can't make all the wood wedges you'll ever need with a few fast swipes of the chain saw. But make the wedges before you start making any cuts where the chain saw might get pinched and hung up!

Gloves should be standard equipment when using a chain saw. Any good work glove will do, of course, but a glove with a nonslip palm and some sort of insulation can be a great help during cutting. Some come with a so-called nonslip plastic beading in the palm. Avoid these gloves like the plague because the first drop of oil or gas makes them skid. The insulation helps to absorb some of the vibration you'll get from the saw. Chain saw vibration has caused an affliction among some professional loggers known as "white finger." The exact causes remain hidden, actually, but vibration is thought to be a major contributing factor, especially in cold weather. The disease can be serious and is apparently quite painful as the circulation to the extremities is cut off or cut down.

Hard hats are available all over the place. Select one of a good quality plastic, and make sure it can be adjusted to a comfortable fit.

Fire extinguishers are needed, though few amateur loggers ever bother to bring one along. Many companies, including Kidde, Bernzomatic, and Sears have small extinguishers of the BC class needed for chain saws. Don't use a class A fire extinguisher on any fire on a chain saw (or a fire caused by spilled chain saw fuel or oil). Class A fire extinguishers are suitable only for paper, wood, and some fabric fires. They will cause dangerous shorts when used on electrical fires; they will spread fires started with gas and oil. If a fire extinguisher must be used, start spraying at the fire's base, sweep the base thoroughly, and move into the body of the burning area. Knock the flames down as quickly as possible so that the extinguisher will have some capacity left in case of a flashback.

Good fuel cans are important. The best are of heavy metal with tight sealing spouts. Prices have gone up in the past few years, but a good heavy fuel can should last nearly forever, if not treated too roughly. Try to locate one of the old G.I. style cans, if possible. They have a little extra gasket around the cap and are still the best going.

Use a funnel too. Try to locate one with a fine mesh brass screen. The screen will take out the largest of the lumps headed for your gas tank. Sooner or later every gas can picks up a load of junk. Getting it out before the fuel filter has to catch the load can be a help.

Figure 8-2 shows a File-n-Joint chain sharpening and depth gauge setting tool. This tool (at less than $20) is considerably cheaper than power sharpening tools and takes at least half the work and tedium out of properly sharpening a chain. It also takes a lot of the suspense out of the job because everything is set at the correct angle and held there. Available from Zip-Penn.

Fig. 8-2. A File-N-Joint installed on a chain saw.

Figure 8-3 shows a chain saw inserted in a Mini-Mill. The Mini-Mill is a small, low production accessory, available from Zip-Penn, Sears, and others. It's easy to use, once the basics are figured out, and produces lumber that, while still rough cut, is much smoother than the rough cut stuff turned out by the circular saws in use at sawmills. Figure 8-4 is a drawing of an Alaskan Jr. portable sawmill, also produced by Zip-Penn.

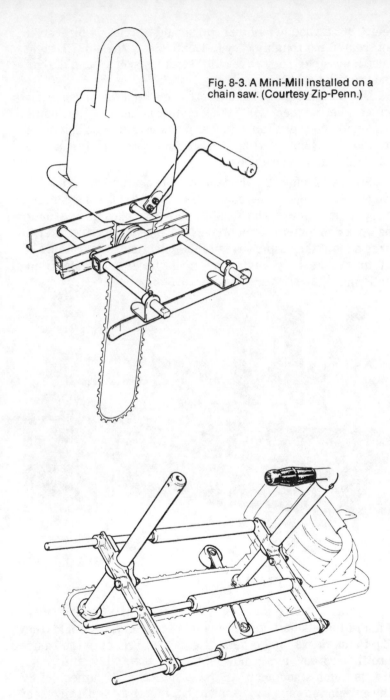

Fig. 8-3. A Mini-Mill installed on a chain saw. (Courtesy Zip-Penn.)

Fig. 8-4. The Alaskan Jr. portable saw mill. (Courtesy Zip-Penn.)

Fig. 8-5. Nail the 2 × 6 to the log to be slabbed.

This is a more expensive, heavy-duty unit, more suitable for the person who wishes to turn out enough lumber to build something as big as a barn. The Mini-Mill goes for about $50 plus shipping, while the Alaskan Jr. is $30 to $40 more, depending on size (according to the guide bar length used). The Mini-Mill will accept any chain saw with a guide bar up to 30 inches in length.

The actual use of a Mini-Mill couldn't be much simpler. First, an aluminum guide rail is screwed to the edge of a 2 × 6. The 2 × 6 is then nailed to the log being slabbed, as shown in Figs. 8-5 and 8-6. The Mini-Mill comes with 2 feet of the guide rail. More can be bought at almost any lumberyard or

191

hardware store, so that the practical length of the planks being cut with this tool is limited only by the length of the logs or the available 2 × 6s.

Figure 8-7 shows the Mini-Mill attached to the chain saw. Figure 8-8 shows the saw and Mini-Mill in action. For slabbing, the ripping guide is left loose, but when the time to make planks comes, that guide is what gives the correct plank thickness (up to about 4 inches).

The Mini-Mill is very easy to handle and not at all fatiguing. The saw and mill is supported by the log being cut, so the weight is off the operator's arms. It is a bit messy, though, as shown in Fig. 8-9. Sawdust is thrown back at the operator, so it would certainly be advisable to wear a pair of safety glasses or goggles to protect your eyes from flying chips.

Figure 8-10 shows what can be done with the Mini-Mill—a 6 × 6 of unseasoned pine.

Fig. 8-6. The Mini-Mill rides on the 2×6.

The Mini-Mill could prove to be a very worthwhile investment for someone who wishes to make a few pieces of outdoor furniture each year, or for someone wanting to build a storage shed. The roughcut wood, of course, is not fine enough for finished cabinet work or indoor furniture, but sanding is easy because of the slightly smoother finish. And there are plenty of planing mills around to take care of that job for those

Fig. 8-7. The aluminum guide rail is attached to the edge of the 2×6.

Fig. 8-8. The Mini-Mill and a chain saw at work.

who need a really smooth finish. The finished lumber has to come out a great deal cheaper than anything you could buy at the local lumberyard. And you can get any size you want, within the limits of the mill, at no extra cost. On top of that, it's really enjoyable to see the grain in your own homemade lumber come out!

Fig. 8-9. A Mini-Mill and saw arrangement throws a lot of sawdust back toward the operator.

Fig. 8-10. The finished product—a 6 × 6 of unfinished pine.

Chapter 9
Using Your Chain Saw

Using Your Chain Saw

Though the modern chain saw is a simple tool to use, it can also be exceptionally dangerous. The chain saw has a rapidly moving series of cutters just hanging right out there waiting to slice through anything in the way. Also most chainsaw use takes place around large trees, and trees never have been and never will be the safest things to slice into when a few sensible rules aren't followed. A chain saw is a powerful tool, a tool that can create forces which might just cause you great problems. The saw pushes and pulls and can kick back very strongly if placed in a cut improperly. Chain saws get the job done, but they can also cause a great deal of grief if not used carefully. So the first rule of chain saw use is "Take the saw seriously. Play it safe."

You should begin considering safety before you even fuel your chain saw. Most of us, over the years, have gotten a bit cavalier in the way we work around gasoline. This can sometimes cause severe injury. A chain saw should be fueled through a funnel, and you must be sure not to slop any of the gas/oil mixture onto hot metal, such as the muffler. Fortunately, most chain saws are designed so that the muffler is well back from the fuel tank, though not completely out of the "splash" area. Any spillage should be wiped from the saw, just as any dirt and sawdust should be wiped from the saw before the fuel cap is removed.

There's yet another reason for trying to prevent chain saw fuel spills. Gasoline and oil do not help the floor of the forest at all. In fact, they can be quite harmful, so keeping the fuel in the tank and the fuel can will be a big help in keeping our forests growing.

Fueling should always be done at least 25 feet from the spot where the saw will be started. Though most chain saws use spark-arresting mufflers today, there's still the chance that a tiny spark will escape and cause an explosion. Those spark-arresting mufflers are designed to pass Forest Service tests which require that nothing large enough to start a fire in the woods can escape. Starting a fire with gasoline is a lot easier than with even the driest leaves. Also if the woods are extremely dry, that day would probably be put to better use in some way other than gathering next winter's firewood.

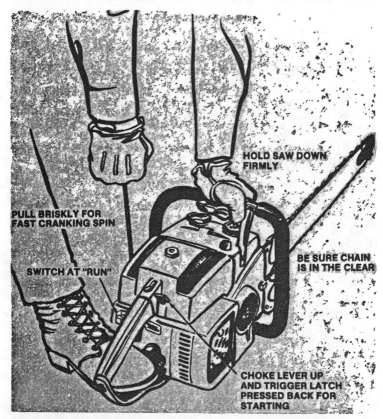

HOLD SAW DOWN FIRMLY

PULL BRISKLY FOR FAST CRANKING SPIN

SWITCH AT "RUN"

BE SURE CHAIN IS IN THE CLEAR

CHOKE LEVER UP AND TRIGGER LATCH PRESSED BACK FOR STARTING

Fig. 9-1. The correct way to hold a chain saw when starting. (Courtesy Homelite.)

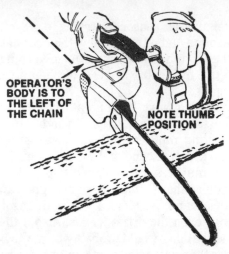

OPERATOR'S BODY IS TO THE LEFT OF THE CHAIN

NOTE THUMB POSITION

Fig. 9-2. Use the proper grip: always keep both hands on the chain saw. (Courtesy Homelite.)

As shown in Fig. 9-1, always make sure the saw is braced and the chain well away from your body when starting the engine. If the saw isn't braced, it can twist around as you yank on the starter cord, with appalling results if the chain strikes any part of the body.

All bystanders should be told to stay out of the cutting or felling area. If trees are being felled, children are especially hard to keep track of and easily miss the dangers of the situation in the thrill of seeing the tree come down. A third party should always take care of any children in the area, with distinct instructions on the safe distances. You'll need your own concentration to keep from injuring yourself or to keep from knocking down power lines or dropping a tree on a building.

Footing should be firm when operating the saw, with the weight of your body well balanced, perferably close to the same on each foot. Cuts should always be made at or below chest level in order to keep control and maintain balance.

A correct, firm grip will help control any chance of kickback and will generally help in correct saw handling. The right hand takes a firm grip on the throttle handle so the saw is well balanced, while the left hand wraps around the handle bar, with the thumb underneath (Fig. 9-2). The thumb webbing, between the thumb and index finger, must be *around* the handle bar. This grip provides the surest control and reduces the chances of your hand slipping into the moving chain.

Stand so that no part of your body is behind the chain while it is moving. In over 93 out of 100 cases, when a chain breaks, it will run off the saw and onto the ground. For those other rare times, you don't want to be on the receiving end. Also there's always the chance the wood you're cutting might contain nails or other debris such as steel shot from guns. Or there's a chance you might tap a rock with the chain. When that happens, it's possible for one or more of the teeth or links to fly off.

More powerful saws pose greater problems for the occasional user because the forces are increased according to the weight and power of the chain saw. Kickback becomes more likely and more dangerous as power increases, as do the push pull forces of normal cutting.

Kickback is the normal reaction of the chain saw when the nose section of the guide bar and chain contact an object (Fig. 9-3). The nose of the guide bar recoils back toward the operator. The easiest way to prevent kickback, or to minimize it, is to consciously keep the nose of the saw from making

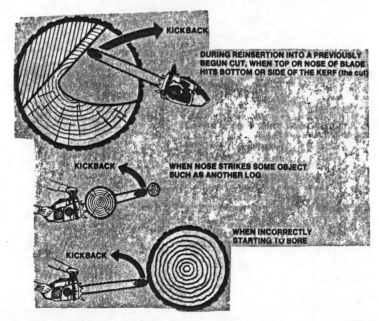

Fig. 9-3. Kickback occurs anytime the nose contacts an object. (Courtesy Homelite.)

contact with any object, including nearby branches and twigs of seemingly modest size. Make cuts well back on the straight portion of the bar whenever possible. A sharp and correctly adjusted chain also cuts down on the chance of severe kickback. Use care when cutting through springy material, such as brush and small trees, making sure that the nose of the saw stays clear of the material around the cut.

Boring cuts, in which the nose of the bar is used to start a cut and continue on through the wood, are handy in some types of cutting, but extreme care should be used even after a great deal of experience is gained in making this type of cut. Always be alert for kickback during boring cuts.

The need for boring may come up when some obstruction prevents placing the saw across the wood, or keeps you from continuing through with a top cut, or prevents your getting underneath the log to relieve stresses with an underbuck (Fig. 9-4). Boring cuts are also handy for cutting blind holes, such as those in rail fences, and those used for cutting out log cabin windows.

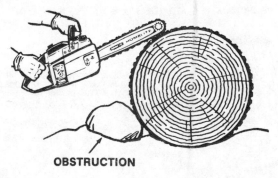

OBSTRUCTION

Fig. 9-4. Sometimes a boring cut is used to get around an obstruction. (Courtesy Homelite.)

As Figure 9-5 shows, the best way to make a boring cut is to make the first contact with the wood as far back from the nose of the bar as possible. Make an angular cut, and when the cut has become deep enough to serve as a guide, exert slight downward pressure to bring the bar slowly into line for boring on through the log. Continue the boring cut until the saw is either through the wood or up to the depth of the bar. When the bar is in deep enough, you can then cut upward or downward through the wood as needed.

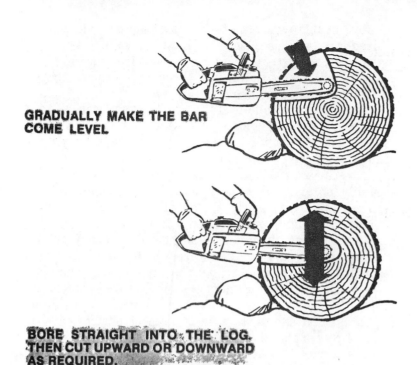

GRADUALLY MAKE THE BAR
COME LEVEL

BORE STRAIGHT INTO THE LOG.
THEN CUT UPWARD OR DOWNWARD
AS REQUIRED.

Fig. 9-5. Making a boring cut. (Courtesy Homelite.)

A point to consider when thinking of making boring and plunge cuts is the rapid wear on both bar and chain caused by this type of cutting. Because of the small area of the saw and guide bar used during boring, the wear is several times more rapid than it is when either the top or bottom flat guide bar areas are used.

Pull is the effect you'll notice when making any top or side cut with the bottom section of the bar. The operator of the saw is pulled forward, toward the saw and the log being cut. Push is just the reverse and occurs with bottom cuts and any other cuts in which the top of the guide bar is used. Maintenance of balance is of great importance in resisting these forces. Make certain your stance is correct, with as close to equal bodyweight distribution as possible. The saw bumper or spikes can be brought into contact with the wood to reduce push or pull forces, though the forces won't be eliminated. Keep watch on the cutting. As soon as the push or pull force stops at the instant the cut is completed, the throttle must be shut down so you can regain or maintain your balance.

Most of this resistance to forces should be done with as relaxed a body as possible. With most homeowner saws, the power is not so extreme that great tension is needed to resist push and pull forces. However, kickback remains an extreme danger with even the smallest chain saws.

Clothing worn while operating a chain saw can be very important. It should fit closely, but not too tightly, allowing for quick movement but staying close enough to the body to be out of the way of the chain and any branches around the cutting site. No scarves, mufflers, or jewelry should be worn. Shoes should be sturdy, with nonslip soles. Good work gloves with nonslip palms are a big help. Though many people hate to work with gloves on, there are two good reasons for everyone using them when using a chain saw. First, when doing heavy cutting, you may have to adjust the chain every half hour or so, and it's razor sharp when in good shape. The bar and chain will often be very hot during adjustments. Second, chain saws vibrate vigorously (even those with the newest antivibration measures) and can cause a large crop of blisters on your hands. A pair of gloves will do much to prevent the blisters.

Eye protection during chain saw operation is very important. If you wear glasses, make certain they have safety lenses. Even then, a pair of safety goggles is worthwhile protection. If you don't wear safety glasses, wear safety goggles at all times when operating your chain saw.

A hard hat should be worn when working under large trees, whether there *seem* to be loose branches above or not. A "widowmaker" or loose branch high up and unseen, can fall with tremendous force—enough force to injure or kill you! Leave the tree standing if you can't shake down *every* sizeable branch that appears even a bit wobbly.

Wearing ear plugs or other hearing protectors is an excellent precaution against loss of hearing. The Mickey Mouse style protectors seen around airports are about the best available, but some of the disposable waxed cotton plugs do a good job too.

Even though most of the work is done by the chain saw and motor, your own physical condition is important to safe chain saw operation. For those of us who have developed our fair share of flab over the sedentary years, the amount of effort needed to control a chain saw will come as a surprise. Take it easy until you work those muscles into decent shape. You need to be relaxed but alert in order to maintain safe working conditions, so getting over tired is one of the worst things you can do. Take a break anytime you feel a bit fatigued.

Don't drink. Don't use drugs that might affect your balance. A check with your doctor or pharmacist if you have to take medication will provide this information. Anything that affects coordination or judgment should be avoided.

If you have, or think you might have, any heart ailment, high blood pressure, or any other serious physical problem, check with your doctor before getting involved in extensive chain sawing operations. While the exercise might just be good for you, it might also be just the little bit needed to push things over the edge. Make sure before starting.

Of course if you're doing a lot of cutting in the woods, extra fuel and chain oil should be brought along. The chain oil can easily be carried in its original 1 quart or 1 gallon container, usually a plastic pour jug. For any extensive woodcutting, bring along at least a quart, for if you run out you'll have to stop cutting until you get more. Fuel should be carried in a metal safety can, premixed and ready to go. Follow the oil manufacturer's directions for a proper mixture.

For safety in carrying the chain saw, a chain cover can be used, as can a case for the entire saw, which comes with some brands and models. The cases tend to be flimsy, so they should be handled with care.

Plastic, wooden, or aluminum wedges can be essential if you misjudge the stresses on a cut and the tree clamps down on your guide bar. Never use a hard surface wedge to free a guide bar. Even with the soft wedges, try not to hit the guide bar when freeing things up.

If you have a roller nose guide bar on the chain saw, you should bring along a filled grease gun to keep the nose rolling free during heavy cutting.

An extra spark plug and the proper size wrench can be a help. In any case, you'll need to bring along a wrench to loosen the guide bar for adjustment and a 6 inch by 3 inch screwdriver to make the adjustment. Most saws provide a combination tool which does all these jobs, from the spark plug to the adjustment.

A fire extinguisher is a good idea even in wet woods. During fall dry spells its an essential for your own and others safety. Use a dry chemical or CO_2 model suitable for oil and grease fires. It will also do a fair job of putting out leaf fires.

Optional equipment can include extra air filters, a sharp axe or hatchet (single blade style), and chain filing tools. A small shovel can help in clearing away dirt from the bottom of logs too large to roll over for the final cut. The shovel can also be an aid should a fire start. If extra chains are brought along, it would pay also to bring along an extra drive sprocket or two. If you spend a lot of time cutting seasoned firewoods, such as oak, you're almost certain to dull at least one chain during a hard day's cutting, and sprockets should be changed whenever chains are changed.

A first aid kit should also be carried along. Small snake bite kits, such as those made by Cutter, can be a safety factor. While contact with a snake is unlikely, there are few areas of the United States totally free of poisonous reptiles. Ankle high boots and a bit of care are the best defenses against snakebite.

Making cuts with a chain saw is a fairly simple operation, but these are some things that should be kept in mind. First, all cuts should be made with full throttle. Cutting at partial throttle will allow the clutch to slip and burn, wearing it out early or providing a quick glaze on the clutch friction surfaces which leads to even more slipping and burning.

When small logs are cut, the throttle should be opened just before the chain touches the wood. If possible, the saw bumper should be right up against the wood. This reduces any push or pull force felt by the saw's operator. Exert only a light feed pressure on the saw to cut straight on through wood, and be ready to release the throttle the instant the chain breaks through the wood. Don't let the saw run wide open without a cutting load because this wears the engine, bar, and chain unnecessarily.

Small logs, as shown in Figure 9-6, can be cut straight on through, even if the bumper can't be placed against the log.

When bucking or felling larger logs and trees, the saw bumper should be placed up against the wood so you can pivot

Fig. 9-6. Cutting small logs. (Courtesy Homelite.)

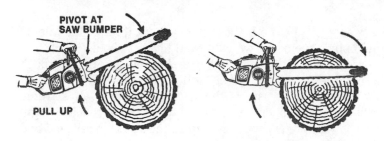

Fig. 9-7. Pivoting the saw through the wood works better on large logs. (Courtesy Homelite.)

the saw at the bumper for best control and easiest feeding (Fig. 9-7).

At no time should the chain at the top or nose section of the bar touch the ground or any object other than the log or branch being cut. Touching the ground will damage the chain; contact with the nose of the bar can cause kickback.

There are two chain saw cuts which deserve special attention: overbucking and underbucking. The definitions are simple enough: with an overbuck, you cut down into the log from the top; with an underbuck, you cut up into a log from underneath. Some logs can be cut with just an overbuck or just an underbuck, but others will require both techniques to keep the guide bar from being pinched as the log stresses close up the cut.

Remember wood is heavy and it bends or flexes. As you cut through a log, you weaken it at the cut and it will bend *there* unless it is lying flat on the ground and under no stress. To avoid closing the cut and pinching the saw blade, therefore, you must cut a stressed log or limb in such a way that the cut will open instead of closing on the bar. In addition, you may wish to avoid splitting the wood or stripping off the bark. If a

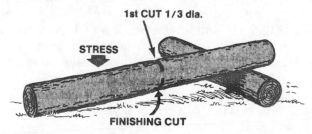

Fig. 9-8. Because of stress, some logs have to be cut from two directions. (Courtesy Homelite.)

log is supported at both ends, an overbuck through the middle would pinch the bar. Two cuts would have to be used: first an overbuck (about 1/3 through the log), then an underbuck through the remaining 2/3 of the log (Fig. 9-8). The overbuck will relieve the stress. If the log doesn't have an extreme amount of end support, it can sometimes be overbucked on an angle so that the cut will open up as the stress is relieved and the log settles (Fig. 9-9).

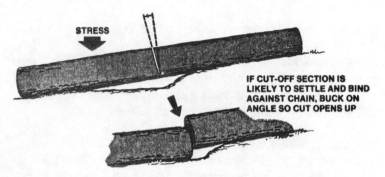

Fig. 9-9. Sometimes logs can be bucked at an angle. (Courtesy Homelite.)

When limbing and pruning, attention must also be paid to stresses. Most limbs should have a starting underbuck, with the finishing cut coming the final two-thirds of the way down from the top. With limbs on living trees, the prevention of splitting back to the trunk or to healthy wood is especially important. So it's usually wise to start the cut some distance out from the trunk, do the underbucking and overbucking, and then lop off the stub with a finishing cut close to the trunk (Fig. 9-10).

When limbing a felled tree, the limbs should be cut from the side opposite that on which you are standing, whenever possible (Fig. 9-11). Unless the tree is a real monster, no cuts should be made while standing on the tree. If some supporting limbs are left uncut, the log will be easier to buck. The supporting limbs can be cut off after bucking.

On standing timber, pruning and limbing should be followed by a painting of preservative so the bark can grow back over the wound (Fig. 9-12).

Basic notching and felling of trees is fairly simple in spite of all the seeming complexities involved. First check for

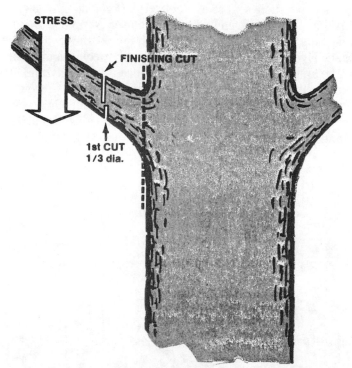

STRESS

FINISHING CUT

1st CUT
1/3 dia.

Fig. 9-10. Limbing a living tree. (Courtesy Homelite.)

nearby trees that might cause the tree you're felling to hang up as it falls. Sooner or later a tree you cut will probably hang up, and you'll then realize how dangerous this problem can become. You never know when the hung tree can break loose. Should a tree become a hanger, the best thing is to leave it be. Of course, that's not always possible. The hanging tree may be a danger to others, or you may need to clear a way.

If the tree stays hung up, a block and tackle should be used, in conjunction with another tree, to pull it down. When attaching the block and tackle to the hung tree, be extremely careful not to get into the path of the tree's fall. The best bet is usually to weight the rope and then toss it over the branch near the spot where you have to pull. Staying well clear, pull the rope under and around the tree, make any needed ties, thread through the pulleys, and go to it.

Check for the presence of power lines, even out in the woods. I've found power lines in the oddest spots imaginable, so a check is *always* needed. Someone surely won't be happy if you yank down their source of electricity. If you do pull down a power line, clear the area and call the power company. Do not continue cutting around it, and don't try to move the line yourself. Even house service lines require special equipment to handle and can be exceptionally dangerous to the layman.

Now, take a look around the base of the tree. If you're lucky, the tree is on level ground and there are clear fall paths all around. Select as natural a fall line as you can. The easiest tree to fell is always the one that can be dropped on its natural fall line.

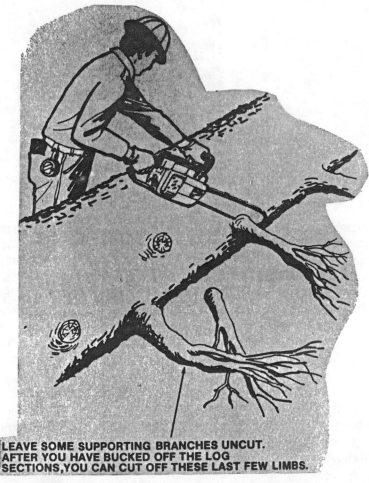

LEAVE SOME SUPPORTING BRANCHES UNCUT. AFTER YOU HAVE BUCKED OFF THE LOG SECTIONS, YOU CAN CUT OFF THESE LAST FEW LIMBS.

Fig. 9-11. When limbing a felled tree, stand on one side of the tree and cut on the other. (Courtesy Homelite.)

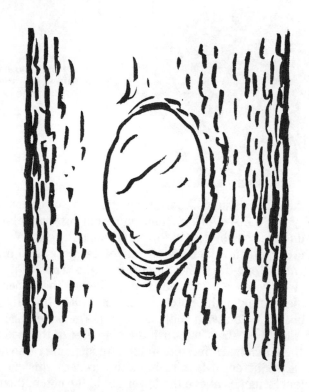

Fig. 9-12. When branches are trimmed neatly flush with the trunk, and the wound is painted with a preservative, the bark can grow back over the cut. (Courtesy Homelite.)

Now, choose your line of retreat. What is wanted is a retreat at about a 45 degree angle to the rear of the tree's fall line (Fig. 9-13) The first chore is to clear that path. Make sure the brush is cleared away and that any loose rocks are moved out so you won't stumble or fall as you retreat.

By the way, a tree may seem to lean a little in one direction, but it may also have several exceptionally heavy limbs on the opposite side. Consider those limbs when you're doing your fall line figuring; they will have a definite affect on the tree's direction as it falls.

Wind velocity, especially when the tree has many branches, can also have a strong effect on the direction of fall.

If the tree is dead, you'll also need to take into consideration the soundness of the trunk. If the tree is hollow, there's a good chance it's a bit more hollow on one side than it

Fig. 9-13. Insure that you have a clear path of retreat when felling a tree. (Courtesy Homelite.)

is on the other. This will definitely affect the direction of fall. Usually you'll discover any hollowness during your felling cut. Examine the possibilities before continuing the cut.

Cutting down a tree usually involves more than one cut. First, about one-third the diameter of the trunk (Fig. 9-14). The lower notch cut is always made before the upper notch cut. The center of the notch should be aimed directly at the area in which you wish the tree to fall. The wide edge of the notch should be about one-fifth the diameter of the tree trunk. Once the notch is completed and the wood chunk removed, the backcut is started. It is parallel to the ground. This cut should be at least 2 inches above the lower cut of the notch, though for large trees the distance can be opened up to a lot more (Fig. 9-14).

As the backcut is being made you should be paying attention to the actions of the tree. If it seems to be settling

Fig. 9-14. Usually, felling a tree involves these cuts. (Courtesy Homelite.)

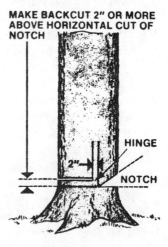

MAKE BACKCUT 2" OR MORE ABOVE HORIZONTAL CUT OF NOTCH

HINGE

2"

NOTCH

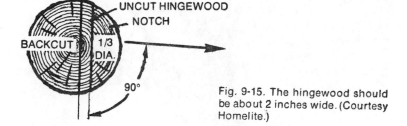

Fig. 9-15. The hingewood should be about 2 inches wide. (Courtesy Homelite.)

back onto the backcut, which is usually indicated by a binding saw, then the tree may not fall in the direction planned. Soft wedges can be driven into the backcut to free the saw. But a careful eye should be kept on the tree anyway, and the wedges should hereafter be kept as tight in the cut as possible in order to tilt the tree in the planned direction of fall.

The backcut should be stopped when there is about a 2 inch chunk of uncut wood holding the trunk (Fig. 9-15). This hinge of uncut wood serves to keep the tree on line as it falls, providing more control (Fig. 9-16). A tree with no hingewood falls almost uncontrollably.

As soon as the tree starts to fall, the saw should be dropped and you should take off along your escape route. Leaving the saw behind may seem a bit extreme, but a chain saw even without a running engine is nothing to be carrying when you're in a hurry. Taking the time to shut off the engine might get you slapped by the tree butt ripping free of its hingewood. The larger the tree, the more likely it is to kick back and the farther it can kick back. Some large trees may kick back as much as 12 feet, and some very large ones as much as 24 feet! That area is no place to be when the butt comes through.

Felling a tree against its natural line of fall poses a few more problems, problems which require some care to safely overcome.

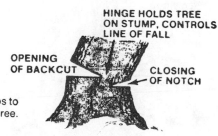

HINGE HOLDS TREE ON STUMP, CONTROLS LINE OF FALL

OPENING OF BACKCUT

CLOSING OF NOTCH

Fig. 9-16. The hingewood helps to control the fall of the tree. (Courtesy Homelite.)

LEANER

Fig. 9-17. Sometimes a leaner must be cut with a special technique. (Courtesy Homelite.)

Probably the nastiest trees to handle are those leaners found on the sides of windy hills (Fig. 9-17). If the lean is extreme enough, no technique will bring the tree down against its natural line of fall. If at all possible, leaners should be felled along their natural line of fall. Even then the stresses present some problems.

A standard hinge, a single notch, and a normal backcut will often leave a stump that is barber chaired (Fig. 9-18). To prevent this, start with a normal notch in the downhill face of

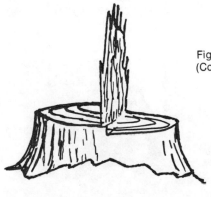

Fig. 9-18. Barber chair stump. (Courtesy Homelite.)

the tree. Follow up with cut number 2, a smaller side notch (Fig. 9-19). Then make cut number 3, another small notch (both the small notches should reach no further in than the sapwood) on the opposite side. Finally, the backcut is made in the normal manner. The first notch should be made as deeply as possible, just up to the point where there's no chance of getting the saw bound in the undercut. A saw bound in an undercut is a real problem. A second saw is almost always needed to cut it loose, with resulting damage to one or both tools.

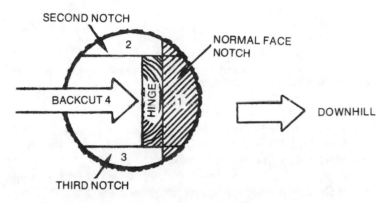

Fig. 9-19. Sometimes special cuts are needed to prevent a barber chair stump. (Courtesy Homelite.)

For felling a more normally situated tree away from its natural line of fall, a couple of felling, or soft, wedges are needed. The first notch is cut as usual. After the notch is cut, the backcut is started, but the end of the hinge closest to the desired line of fall is left thicker than the other end (Fig. 9-20). The wedges are driven into the backcut in line with the desired direction of fall and are kept as tight as possible until the tree starts to go.

In more extreme cases, a block and tackle, or at least a single pulley arrangement may be needed. The block and tackle allows the second person to apply a great deal more strength, but is more complicated to set up. Usually a block and tackle is necessary when the line of fall must be close to exact to miss power lines, houses, and other obstructions. Figure 9-21 shows the arrangement needed to get the leverage necessary to pull the tree in the desired direction. The rope

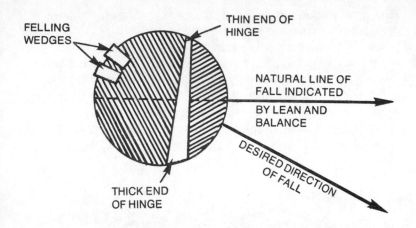

Fig. 9-20. The hingewood must be wider at one end if the tree is to fall away from its natural line of fall. (Courtesy Homelite.)

handler must stand at least twice the tree height away, for the tree will be falling right in his direction. Tree height is easy to misjudge, and it's better to be safe than sorry. The higher up the tree the rope can be tied, the better.

When you run into a tree too large to be cut with a single pass of the chain saw, special techniques can be a great help. A series of cuts, as shown in Fig. 9-22, provide the extra depth needed. As shown, the first cut is made by pivoting the bar into the cut, starting on either side of the trunk. The same technique is used on both notch cuts, though the saw can then

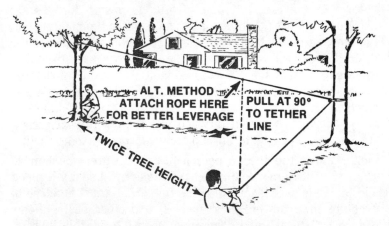

Fig. 9-21. A block and tackle arrangement can sometimes be used to control the direction of fall. (Courtesy Homelite.)

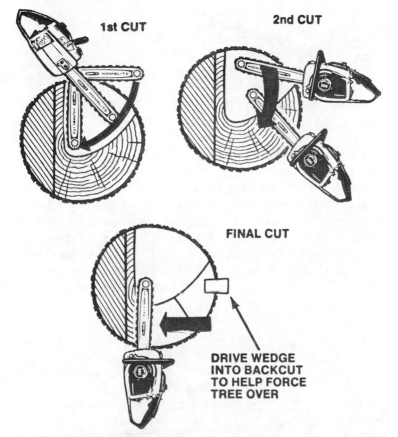

1st CUT

2nd CUT

FINAL CUT

DRIVE WEDGE
INTO BACKCUT
TO HELP FORCE
TREE OVER

Fig. 9-22. A series of cuts are needed to make the backcut on very large trees. (Courtesy Homelite.)

usually be drawn through the cut since it's not as deep as the backcut. The hinge section is left as with any other backcut. The saw is then removed and it's position reversed for the second cut, though here you must make certain the throttle is wide open. Reinsert the saw carefully to prevent kickback. Finally, the saw is drawn forward into the cut to reach the hinge and complete the felling. In trees this large, wedges will almost *always* be needed to hold the backcut open and to tilt the tree towards the notch and the direction of fall desired.

Once the tree is on the ground, pruning and bucking take place. One problem likely to arise at this point will be the spring pole. As your tree falls, it may trap saplings underneath (Fig. 9-23). A sapling under tension like this is called a spring

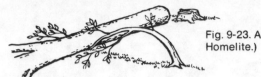

Fig. 9-23. A spring pole. (Courtesy Homelite.)

pole. If at all possible, these spring poles should be worked around during limbing and bucking. When the tree has been bucked into small sections, the spring poles will be automatically released when the bucked log is rolled off them. When they are not automatically defused, a bit of study should show the direction of whip to be expected from the spring pole, and the pole can then be cut with the chain saw so it can't hit anyone. It is better, though, to buck the tree and then roll the logs off the spring pole. This is a much safer procedure because it's always possible to misjudge the direction of whip. Though a sapling doesn't sound all that dangerous, there's a lot of energy stored in that 1 or 2 inch trunk when it's bent over!

Fig. 9-24. Cutting logs on a sawhorse. (Courtesy Homelite.)

For log bucking on a sawhorse, the log can be drawn over the sawhorse and cut off with no worry about stresses (Fig. 9-23). The short lengths being cut have minimal stresses and will just drop free as they're cut through. Cut on uphill side only.

Chapter 10
Chain Saws
And Firewood

Chain Saws And Firewood

Though chain saws can do all sorts of cutting jobs well, the most usual use of the tool today is in cutting firewood for wood stoves and fireplaces (Fig. 10-1). A cheerful and blazing wood fire today has also become a major money saving way to heat houses.

An average size homeowner's chain saw logging operation can save from 10 to 50 percent of most home heating bills each year. At that rate, it doesn't take long to pay for a $200 chain saw. Often a single season or less will do the job. The average homeowner's saw will provide about 500 BTUs worth of heat energy for each single BTU of gasoline energy needed to power the saw. So more and more homeowners are going back to at least part-time wood heat.

Wood is not as hard to find as most people might imagine. While the most desirable woods for fuel may well be hard to locate in some areas, there is almost no area in the United States and Canada where some sort of fuel wood is not available. Often the availability is simply a matter of making yourself familiar with locales where firewood can be found. The luckiest homeowner will have a woodlot of his own, but most of us will have to do some checking and chasing to locate the spots to cut the wood we need.

Fortunately, there are sufficient forests in nearly all areas, so location is not difficult. The first check should be

Fig. 10-1. Cutting wood for burning.

made with state and federal foresters in your area. Many state and national forestlands allow controlled cutting of downed and dead timber in an effort to help increase forest growth. (Proper cropping of almost any woodlot will add a great deal to its productive capacity over a period of years, so this is something to keep in mind even when working on your own woodland.) Permits are granted and the recommendations and rules must be followed.

The private woodland is another source of firewood. Check with farmers and others in your locale who may want their timber thinned or need dead and fallen trees cut out. Talk over the situation with the owner. If the only requirement is to keep your cutting to downed timber, stay with that condition. In other cases, the owner may wish to charge a few dollars stumpage fee for you to cut down standing timber. If this is the case, make sure there's an agreement on the size and kind of trees you can cut for the fee. The fee most often will range from $1 a cord up to as much as $5, but the stricter the woodlot owner's requirements for kinds of wood cut, the lower the fee must be. In any case, don't leave a mess of trimmed branches sitting in a pile or scattered over the forest floor. These trimmings are a fine source of kindling for your fires. A mass of dead branches over the forest floor can constitute a fire hazard.

Another spot to check when searching out firewood is the local dump. U.S. Forest Service figures indicate that at least 30 percent of the landfill going into most dumps is waste wood from trimming projects, land clearing, and such jobs. The dump operators should be happy to have you remove as much as you can since problems crop up as soon as any landfill area is full. Though in some parts of the country you may have to pay a fee, you should resist as strongly as possible since you are actually doing the operator a favor by keeping the landfill from becoming full too soon.

When you locate woodland, sometimes it's a good idea to see if a state or national forester can come in and mark the trees that should be removed. In most, if not all, states, the state forestry service will provide this service for nothing. In fact, in several states some forestland qualifies for a payment from the state or federal government if the land is cropped according to the forester's recommendations. Though the fee is low (about $5 an acre), it's all money off the fuel bill because you'd likely be doing the work anyway. If any woodlot owner has doubts about your cutting on his land, check with the forestery service to see if they'll mark the marketable timber so it won't be cut down.

When the logs are ready for splitting, there are a few things to be done. First, you'll need some tools. Some people prefer an axe for splitting wood, others a woodsplitter's maul. If an axe is used, select one with a thick heel to spread the wood as it moves through the split. *Never* drive an axe through wood with a hammer, and *never* use the axe to drive a splitting wedge into the wood.

For those who prefer a woodsplitter's maul, the job is a bit simpler. A woodsplitter's maul looks something like a sledgehammer with an axe on one side. Actually, the wedged side is just that: wedged. It is not nearly as sharp as an axe, though it does need to have a reasonably sharp edge. With such a maul and two or three splitting wedges, almost any log that can be split will split. Splitting wedges differ from bucking and felling wedges in that they are made of steel—and are usually quite a bit larger.

The easier-to-split logs can be split with the maul alone, using the wedged end and just letting the weight of the 6 pound or so head carry the maul through the wood. Try to hit a natural split line in the wood. Easily split woods, such as the maples, pines, and others will usually require no wedges to finish the split. Hard-to split woods, such as seasoned oak, may require wedges. When a wedge is used, it should be tapped into a natural split line with the blunt side of the maul. The maul is lifted and dropped on the wedge, which should then split the wood with little difficulty. Again, no power beyond the natural fall of the maul is necessary. Too many people overwork themselves and increase their chances of various kinds of injury by slamming the maul or an axe down as hard as they can swing. Just let its own weight do the work and you'll split more wood with less effort.

When the wood is split, stacking and seasoning become the problem. Wood should not be stacked in tight ricks, or piles. Many woods will rot before they air-dry when stacked in that manner. Since air-dried wood is desirable, proper stacking is necessary to get the wood dry as quickly as possible. Air-dried wood almost always has more heat value than wood that has not been air-dried. If wood is air-dried for 6 months the heat value increases to 93 percent of the heat value of wood seasoned for a year; wood seasoned for 3 months has 85 percent of the heat value of 100 percent dry wood. (Actually, fully air-dried wood is wood that has been seasoned to a 20 to 25 percent moisture content, so it cannot really be considered 100 percent dry. Keeping a supply of wood in the house can cut the moisture content to well below 25 percent.)

Figure 10-2 shows the proper way to stack wood for the best seasoning results. This is known as a chimney stack and results in increased air circulation, allowing for quicker seasoning and less rot.

Fig. 10-2. A chimney stack.

Start the stack by laying either waste logs or flat rocks on the ground. Next, lay another row of logs across the first two. Continue this process as high as is safe. Foot long stove lengths, after splitting, will stack to about 3 feet without toppling over too easily, while longer lengths will go up farther, often to twice that height.

When the stack is completed, a board, flat rock, or piece of plastic can be used to cover the top of the stack to keep out rain and snow. After seasoning is completed, the wood can be moved to a woodshed, barn, or other weather protected area.

If wood is cut during the winter, while sap flow is stopped or slowed, 6 months seasoning is usually sufficient. With luck, you'll be able to cut dead wood and thus reduce seasoning time to a month or so.

Remember that split wood seasons much quicker than unsplit. Some woods, such as paper birch, are almost certain to rot before seasoning unless they are split first because the bark forms an exceptionally tight seal. Bark is also a natural insulator, making it harder to start a fire with a log with the bark on than with a split log. If the bark is stripped and dried, it then becomes an excellent kindling.

Logs that are more than 10 inches in diameter should be split in half; logs over 14 inches in diameter should be quartered.

When looking for wood, there isn't a single "right" wood to use for all types of fires. Most conifers, or softwoods, are resinous and can cause heavy creosote deposits in chimneys of wood stoves and fireplaces, increasing the dangers of a chimney fire. A fire kept blazing hot will cut down on such deposits, though. Most deciduous trees, or hardwoods, have higher fuel, or heat, values per cord than do softwoods because of their greater density (though some so-called hardwoods are actually less dense than are many softwoods).

The density of hardwoods can vary a great deal. A cord of air-dried white oak, a hardwood, will weigh (assuming a total of 90 cubic feet per cord and about 20 percent moisture content) about 5130 pounds. Shagbark hickory, also a hardwood, will weigh about 5670 pounds per cord. Butternut, or white walnut, another hardwood, will weigh about 2700 pounds per cord. Butternut weighs about the same as the middle range softwoods.

For the best woodburning, mixed woods are needed. A resinous wood such as pine or cedar makes fire starting a lot easier, but the fire builds faster with one of the less dense hardwoods. For a lasting, intense fire, the oaks and hickories are about as good as you can get. There are heavier woods, but most of them are hard to find, or the trees come in such small sizes you'll spend half your life looking for enough for a single winter's fuel.

The following is a list of common woods and some of their characteristics.

SOFTWOODS

arborvitae—Also called northern white cedar. This aromatic tree is very light, with a cord of wood weighing only

2100 pounds. It will reach 60 feet with a trunk up to 2 feet thick. Easily split. It burns very rapidly.

eastern hemlock—Reaches 60 to 70 feet with a 2 to 3 foot trunk diameter. It is easily split and burns quickly. Weighs about 2700 pounds per cord.

eastern red cedar—A medium weight wood, weighing nearly 3300 pounds per cord. Easily split. It is resinous and quick burning. Mature trees seldom exceed 40 feet, with a 2 foot trunk diameter.

common juniper—An aromatic wood weighing about 2800 pounds per cord. It is seldom thick enough to split since the mature trees are only about 24 feet tall. Rapid burning and resinous. Juniper provides gins with their characteristic flavor.

jack pine—Also known as scrub pine or black pine. Splits easily and burns quickly. This resinous tree may reach 60 to 80 feet with a 2 foot trunk diameter. A cord will weigh about 3150 pounds.

loblolly pine—Also called Indian pine. One of the heavier pines, with a cord weighing about 4100 pounds. Resinous. It splits easily and burns quickly. A mature tree is 90 to 110 feet tall with a 2 to 3 foot trunk diameter.

northern balsam—Also known as silver pine. Easily split and fast burning. Weight about 2800 pounds per cord. The resinous mature tree will reach 40 to 60 feet with a trunk no more than 2 feet thick.

pitch pine—Also called sap pine. It splits easily and burns rapidly, producing a lot of heat. Resinous. The pitch pine will stand from 40 to 60 feet tall, with 1 to 2 foot trunk diameter. The wood weighs about 3700 pounds per cord.

red pine—Also called hard, or Norway pine. Normal growth of this resinous tree reaches 60 to 80 feet with a 2 foot trunk diameter. Easily split, burns quickly, weighs about 3600 pounds per cord.

southern balsam—Similar to the northern balsam.

southern white cedar—Also known as swamp cedar. Extremely light, weighing no more than 2200 pounds per cord. Easily split. It burns rapidly and is resinous. Mature trees are large, rising to 120 feet, with 5 foot trunk diameters.

tamarack—Also known as the American black, or red, larch. Another heavy softwood, weighing about 4100 pounds per cord. It is resinous and burns quickly. Splits easily. The mature tree can reach 60 feet with a 1 to 2 foot trunk diameter.

white pine—Also called soft pine. Normally growing to 60 or 80 feet with a 2 to 3 foot trunk, the white pine is resinous and weighs about 2700 pounds per cord. Easily split.

white spruce—Weighs about 2700 pounds per cord. Easily split and rapid burning. Resinous. The mature tree will stand 60 to 70 feet tall, with a trunk 1 1/2 to 2 feet in diameter.

HARDWOODS

American beech—A fine fuel but is exceptionally hard to split. Weighs about 4700 pounds per cord. It is slow burning. Mature trees will reach 80 feet, with trunks up to 3 feet in diameter.

American linden—Also called basswood. A very light wood at about 2700 pounds per cord. Splitting is easy, but it makes a poor fuel because it burns too quickly. A mature basswood can reach 80 feet, with a 3 foot trunk diameter.

apple—Fine fuel producers. Most of the trees are small, but the wood is heavy, usually over 4500 pounds per cord. Easily split and beautifully aromatic.

black ash—Also called hop, basket, or water ash. It weighs about 4300 pounds per cord and is very easy to split. The mature tree can reach 60 feet, with a 2 foot trunk diameter.

black gum—Also called sour gum or tupelo. It is a middle weight wood of some 4300 pounds per cord, but it is extremely difficult to split. In most cases, the wood will have to be split by running the chain saw up it lengthwise, a job for which most chain saws are not designed. The mature tree will reach as high as 80 feet, with a 3 foot trunk diameter.

blackjack oak—Also called scrub oak. Weighs about 4900 pounds per cord and is easy to split An excellent fuel. The scrub oak is small, reaching no more than 30 feet in height, with a 1 foot trunk diameter.

black locust—Also known as bastard acacia. A heavy wood at 5300 pounds per cord. It is moderately easy to split and makes a good fuel. The mature tree can reach 60 feet, with 2 foot trunk diameter.

black oak—Weighs about 4500 pounds per cord and is easily split. An excellent fuel. The black oak will reach 70 feet in height, with a 3 foot trunk diameter.

blue ash—Weighs about 4860 pounds per cord. Easy to split. The mature tree will stand no more than 50 feet tall, with a 2 foot trunk diameter.

box elder—Also called the sugar ash and is very light for a hardwood at about 2800 pounds per cord. Easily split. Its rapid burning makes it a poor to fair fuel. The mature tree will reach 75 feet, with a trunk as thick as 4 feet.

broom hickory—Also called pignut. An exceptionally heavy wood, weighing about 5800 pounds per cord. It is a hard-to-start but otherwise fine fuel wood. It's tough to split. The mature pignut will reach as much as 80 feet in height with a 2 foot trunk diameter.

butternut—Also called white walnut. An exceptionally light hardwood with a cord weighing only about 2700 pounds. Easily split. It burns very rapidly, making its fuel rating poor. The mature tree will grow to 60 feet tall with a 2 foot trunk diameter.

chinkapin oak—Also called rock oak. Very heavy, even for an oak, with a cord weighing about 5760 pounds. Moderately hard to split. The mature chinkapin oak can reach 70 feet, with a 3 foot trunk diameter.

white elm—Also called American elm. Has had problems with Dutch elm disease, but in uninfected areas can reach up to 100 feet in height with a 6 foot trunk diameter. This stately tree is an excellent fuel, with a cord weight of nearly 3800 pounds. It is exceptionally difficult to split.

cork elm—Also called rock, hickory, or cliff elm. Weighs about 4700 pounds per cord. It is also hard to split. A mature cork elm can reach 80 feet, with a 3 foot trunk diameter.

cottonwood—Large trees, often reaching 150 feet with 6 foot trunk diameters. The wood is very light for a hardwood, seldom weighing more than 2950 pounds per cord. It is easily split and burns quickly. Its rapid burning keeps cottonwood from being a really good fuel, but it makes a good substitute where other hardwoods are unavailable or in short supply.

eastern ironwood—Also known as rough barked ironwood. Weighs about 5400 pounds per cord. Another excellent, tough-to-split firewood. A small tree, seldom exceeding 40 feet with a 1 foot thick trunk.

eastern white oak—An excellent fuel wood. Heavy at about 5130 pounds per cord. Splits with moderate ease. Mature trees are also large, allowing a lot of the season's cutting to be done in one spot. The mature white oak can reach 100 feet, with a 4 foot trunk diameter.

flowering ash—Also known as the fringe tree. Moderately heavy at 4320 pounds per cord. The mature tree is small, standing no more than 40 feet. Seldom of a diameter that requires splitting.

gray birch—Weighs about 3780 pounds per cord and is moderately easy to split. The mature trees are small, standing only about 20 to 30 feet high.

hickories—All excellent fuels.

mountain maple—Also called the water maple. Similar to the striped maple. Reaching up to about 35 feet in height.

northern red oak—Also called gray oak and is one of the lighter oaks with a cord weighing about 4500 pounds. Moderately easy to split. The mature northern red oak will stand up to 80 feet tall, with a trunk about 4 feet thick.

Ohio buckeye—Also called the fetid, or stinking, buckeye. It is also light for a hardwood, weighing no more than 3060 pounds per cord. Easily split. It is a fair fuel. The mature tree will reach 50 feet, with a 2 foot trunk diameter.

paper birch—Also called canoe birch. At about 4230 pounds per cord, it rates as a bit above medium weight and makes an excellent fuel. It must be split. Otherwise the bark seals so tightly the wood will rot before it seasons properly. Paper birch splits easily, fortunately. Mature trees will reach 70 feet, with 3 foot trunk diameter.

pecan—About the same weight as black hickory, 4860 pounds per cord. It is difficult to split. An excellent fuel. The mature tree can reach 100 feet with a 4 foot trunk diameter. Some huge versions are 180 feet tall with 6 foot trunk diameter.

persimmon—Also called the possumwood or date plum. The wood is very heavy at around 5600 pounds per cord. Splitting effort is moderate but often not needed as the mature persimmon will have a trunk only about 1 foot thick, with tree height ranging from 25 to 50 feet.

pin cherry—Also called the fire cherry and is an aromatic light wood at 3330 pounds per cord. Easily split. The mature pin cherry can reach 40 feet in height with a 20 inch trunk diameter.

pin oak—Weighs about 4500 pounds per cord. Requires moderate splitting effort and can reach 80 feet in height.

post oak—Also known as the iron oak. Its exceptionally heavy wood weighs about 5670 pounds per cord and is not very difficult to split. The mature tree will reach up to 50 feet, with a trunk about 2 feet thick.

red ash—Also known as river, or bastard, ash. In the medium weight range at 4300 pounds per cord. It splits easily and is a good fuel, though the mature tree is rather small, ranging from 30 to 50 feet in height, with a 1 to 2 foot thick trunk.

red maple—Also known as the swamp or scarlet, maple. It is medium heavy at 4100 pounds per cord. Easily split. This is one of the largest maples, with the mature tree reaching up to 90 feet, with a trunk 3 1/2 feet thick.

river birch—Also called red, or black, birch. Moderately heavy at 4300 pounds per cord. A good fuel. River birch splits with moderate ease. Mature trees can reach 70 feet in height, with 2 foot trunk diameter.

scarlet oak—About the same weight per cord as is the northern red oak, 4500 pounds. Moderately easy to split. It is an excellent fuel wood, with the mature tree reaching up to 80 feet and 3 feet in diameter.

shagbark hickory—Also known as shellbark hickory and is nearly as heavy as broom hickory at 5670 pounds per cord. It is tough to split. Excellent fuel wood. The mature tree is about the same size as the broom hickory.

silver maple—Also known as soft maple. Weighs about 3600 pounds per cord. It is very easily split, and the mature tree is about the same size as the sugar and black maples.

slippery elm—Also known as red elm. Weighs about 4700 pounds per cord. It is hard to split. The mature tree will reach as high as 70 feet, with a 2 foot trunk diameter.

smoothbarked ironwood—Also known as American hornbeam. It weighs about 5220 pounds per cord. Fuel value is excellent but splitting is difficult. The mature tree is small, seldom surpassing 40 feet with an 18 inch trunk diameter.

striped maple—Also known as the northern maple. Weighs about 3600 pounds per cord. Seldom grows over 25 feet tall, with a trunk only 8 inches thick.

sugar maple—Also called hard, or rock, maple. It is one of the most popular fuel woods in its range. The wood is heavy at 4770 pounds per cord and is easily split when green. The tree is also of good size, providing a lot of wood for a single felling, with mature trees reaching as high as 80 feet, with 3 foot trunk diameters.

swamp post oak—Also called overcup oak. Another very heavy oak, weighing over 5500 pounds per cord. It is a bit more difficult to split than either eastern white oak or post oak, but still makes an excellent fuel wood. The mature tree can reach 60 feet tall, with a 3 foot trunk diameter.

sweet buckeye—Also known as the big buckeye. It is very light as 2700 pounds per cord. Hard to split. Sweet buckeye is a poor fuel. The mature tree will reach 90 feet tall, with a 3 foot trunk diameter.

sweet gum—Also called red gum, gum tree, or alligator wood. It weighs about 4000 pounds per cord and is resinous. Easily split. The resin makes sweet gum a poor to fair fuel wood. The mature tree can reach up to 120 feet, with a 4 foot trunk diameter.

water locust—A moderately heavy wood at 4770 pounds per cord. Moderate splitting effort is needed. The mature tree will grow to 60 feet, with a trunk about 3 feet in diameter.

white ash—Also known as American, or cane, ash. Harder to split than most other ashes, but still only in the moderate splitting effort range. The wood weighs about 4400 pounds per cord, and the mature tree stands about 80 feet tall, with a trunk as thick as 3 feet. A good fuel wood.

white elm—Also called American elm. Has had problems with Dutch elm disease, but in uninfected areas can reach up to 100 feet in height with a 6 foot trunk diameter. The stately tree is an excellent fuel, with a cord weight of nearly 3800 pounds. It is exceptionally difficult to split.

yellow birch—Also known as bitter, silver, or gray birch. It is near the heavy end of the scale with a cord weighing about 4600 pounds. Moderately easy to split. Yellow birch is another wood that must be split to season because the bark makes a very tight seal and will cause rot if not split. Mature trees will reach 80 feet, with 2 foot trunk diameters.

This list is by no means exhaustive. There are literally hundreds of tree species in the United States and Canada which have not been mentioned. Someone, someday will do a book on every form of North American tree suitable for any kind of firewood use, but that day has yet to come. Until recently there just wasn't enough interest. The trees listed are scattered around the country. Most were chosen because they are widespread through most areas of the United States.

Fuel values for the various woods are rather easily figured. Most air-dried wood produces about 7000 BTUs of heat per pound. Resinous woods produce a couple hundred more BTUs per pound because the resin adds to heat production. Simply multiply the weight of a cord by 7000 to get the heat value at 100 percent efficiency. Next, multiply your answer by the heating efficiency of your woodburning appliance, whether stove or fireplace. The answer will be the number of BTUs you can expect from a specific kind of wood used in your woodburning appliance.

Heating efficiency from woodburners is difficult to figure, but most fireplaces can be estimated to extract about 10 percent of the useful heat (heat that actually warms a room) from firewood. The rest goes up the chimney. Some better fireplaces, including those with heat circulating liners, should produce an efficiency rating of at least 15 percent. Improperly cared for fireplaces, by the way, can cause a net heat loss in the home, so fireplace tending becomes very important.

Old style wood stoves, including box stoves, parlor stoves, Franklin stoves, and kitchen ranges can provide an efficiency of 40 to 50 percent.

More modern wood stoves, such as those made by Ashley and Jøtul, can increase efficiency to as high as 65 percent. A 65 percent rating is going to beat all but the best oil- and gas-fired furnaces, which tend to range from 50 percent to 65 percent in efficiency.

So if your wood stove operates on a 50 percent efficiency level, and you're using shagbark hickory for your main firewood, each cord of wood will provide you with over 19 million BTUs of useful heat. The actual BTU output of the cord of wood is about 38 million, but it is cut in half by the 50 percent efficiency rating.

Each gallon of fuel oil for your furnace has about 140,000 available BTUs, so a furnace operating at 60 percent efficiency would result in each gallon of fuel oil giving an actual 84,000 BTUs of heat to the home. At the 19 million BTU mark for the hickory, a cord of hickory would equal 226 gallons of fuel oil. At $.41 per gallon, you would come out equal if the hickory cost you about $90 per cord. At $.51 per gallon, the price of a cord of hickory could rise to $115 and still leave you on an equal basis with fuel oil. Fortunately, if you use your chain saw, the actual cost of a cord of hickory or any other hardwood should be under $10! This price includes cost of chain saw maintenance and repair. The cost of a cord of wood cut with a chain saw won't remain constant, but it will vary little. Softer, lighter woods cause less wear and tear on the chain, but it takes more of the wood to keep the fire going. It all equals out.

By using wood heat, it's possible to save as much as 90 percent on your winter fuel bill. With fuel prices so high, woodburning never looked so good.

I've used adjusted figures in this book to determine the weight of a cord of wood. Though a cord actually is 128 cubic feet, I've considered the lost space from air spaces and so forth and dropped the cord cubic footage down to 90 per cord. The wood weights listed are taken from available information on *dry* wood weight and then 20 percent is added to allow for moisture content. If your cord is more tightly packed or more loosely packed, the weights can differ considerably.

Chapter 11
Chain Saw Projects

Chain Saw Projects

Chain saws were not designed just to cut down trees and cut up cordwood. There are so many things they can be used to make, your imagination is about the only limit. This chapter will take a look at a few basic projects, all of which can be produced in just a short time.

Possibly the handiest additional tool for the chain saw is the sawhorse, or sawbuck. Because you need two hands to use the saw, the sawhorse serves to keep the workpiece from rolling around while you're trying to get some work done on it.

Making a sawhorse is pretty easy. Use light logs, no more than 4 or 5 inches in diameter, and build the sawhorse shown in Fig. 11-1. If you want, you can even construct a portable unit (Fig. 11-2). Both can be built in half an hour or thereabouts, and both can be very handy.

Mailbox posts or supports are handy in suburban areas and essential in rural areas, but most are expensive and hard to put together. The two shown in Figs. 11-3 and 11-4 are simple to make and can be put together in very short order. Installation, as covered in the caption on Fig. 11-4, takes longer but will prove worthwhile. Try to use a wood rated as durable in contact with the ground, such as cedar.

Figure 11-5 shows a bird feeder that can be put together in less than 2 hours, with minimal materials.

Figure 11-6 shows a seesaw that will provide hours of delight for your children. Sink two posts about 5 inches in diameter, about 12 inches apart. Let them stick up about 24

236

Fig. 11-1. A sawhorse made of light logs. (Courtesy Homelite.)

inches. An easy way to do this is to dig a hole big enough to accept both posts. Set them in place, then fill in around them with the dirt, tamping it firmly as you fill. With the posts in place, use your chain saw to cut a groove in the top of each post, as shown. These grooves will accept a length of 1 inch galvanized pipe from the local plumbing shop long enough to span the two posts. Screw regular pipe caps on the ends of the pipe. For the rocker, pick out a good, sound 2 × 12 at the lumberyard. About 12 or 14 feet is long enough. Nail some 1 × 2 cleats to the bottom of the 2 × 12, as shown. These keep the plank from sliding on the pipe and let the kids adjust it when one of them is heavier than the other. Of course, you can make a 2 × 12 using the Mini-Mill, as described in the chapter on accessories.

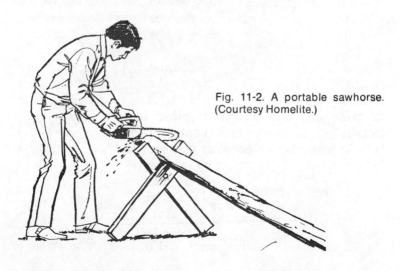

Fig. 11-2. A portable sawhorse. (Courtesy Homelite.)

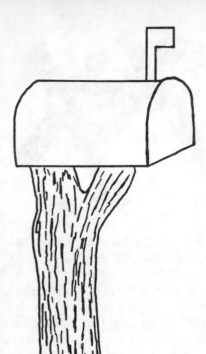

Fig. 11-3. A mailbox post cut with a chain saw. (Courtesy Homelite.)

Your chain saw can even help you build a bunk bed (Fig. 11-7). Four heavy saplings of small trees form the posts for the bed—and a branch stub or two on each post provides a hanging place for such things as bathrobes.

This project takes an easy weekend to build, and calls for very little expensive material. Besides the posts you need:

4—5/4 × 8 inch pine 10 feet long
6—1 × 2 inch pine 10 feet long
32 No. 14 flathead screws 2 1/2 inches long
48 No. 8 flathead screws 1 1/4 inches long
Small bottle of white glue
Paint or stain

To make the project, follow these steps:

1. Cut each of the 5/4 inch × 10 feet boards into a side rail and an end rail. The actual dimensions of these pieces will depend on the size of the boxspring. The standard is 38 × 75 inches *inside*—but check your springs to be sure. Note that the ends lap the sides; keep this in

mind, and add twice the thickness of the stock to the length of the end pieces (Fig. 11-8).

2. Assemble the two frames, using glue and screws. Draw the screws exactly flush with the surface so they will barely show—or make them disappear entirely by countersinking them slightly, then filling the depression with wood plastic. Be sure the two frames are exactly square, then let them sit until the glue is dry.

3. Use your chain saw, as shown in Fig. 11-9, to notch the posts. Make the notch exactly as deep as the side rails are thick and exactly as wide as the width of the boards. First do a series of side-by-side cuts. Then let the saw teeth *gently* ride the surface as you slowly move the saw back and forth across the notch, angling it slightly from side to side as you go.

Fig. 11-4. For a firm footing, dig a hole in the ground about twice the diameter of the post. Set the post in place and brace it temporarily. Fill in around it with concrete. Take the braces off after three days. (Courtesy Homelite.)

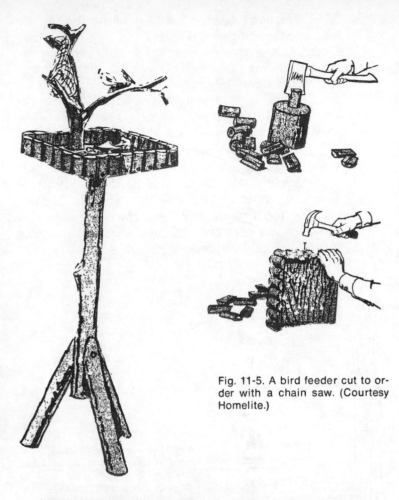

Fig. 11-5. A bird feeder cut to order with a chain saw. (Courtesy Homelite.)

Note: Observe the spacing for the two beds, as indicated in Fig. 11-10. As shown, the spacing provides plenty of room for the occupant of the lower bunk to sit up.

4. Fasten the two frames to the posts with screws, leaving 6 or 8 inches of hangover at both ends.
5. Cut the 1 × 2s to length and use screws and glue to fasten them along the bottom edges of the frames (Fig. 11-11).
6. Cut the remainder of the 1 × 2s into slats to rest across the frames, to provide extra support for the spring.

How about finish? You can stain or paint the boards, as you wish. Also—you can leave the bark on the posts or remove

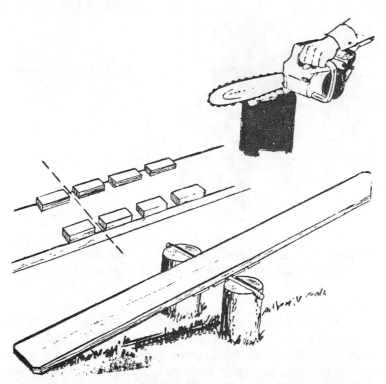

Fig. 11-6. A seesaw can also be a chain saw project. (Courtesy Homelite.)

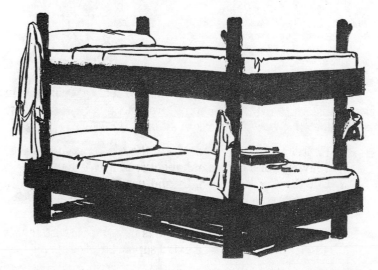

Fig. 11-7. A chain saw can even be used to build a bunk bed. (Courtesy Homelite.)

Fig. 11-8. Add twice the thickness of the stock to the length of end pieces. (Courtesy Homelite.)

it, as you wish. Then, you can even paint the posts if your leaning is less toward rustic than toward pop-modern.

Figure 11-12 shows how to cut discs of wood to lay as a patio surface. Figure 11-13 shows one such finished patio. This could make a good weekend project.

First make the base smooth and level. Then spread a layer of sand and very fine gravel ("pea gravel") about an inch thick. Lay the disks in this bed, adding a little gravel or scooping a little away as may be needed to maintain level. Then, fill the spaces between the disks with more gravel. The

Fig. 11-9. The posts can be notched with your chain saw. (Courtesy Homelite.)

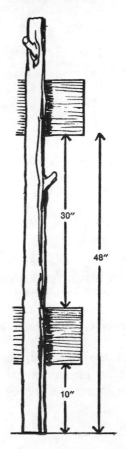

Fig. 11-10. Vertical dimensions for the bunk bed. (Courtesy Homelite.)

easy way to do this is to rake and broom a ridge of gravel across the area from one side to the other. Gradually, it will disappear into the spaces. The next time it rains—or when you sprinkle the area with the hose—the gravel will compact, leaving just the right amount of texture to make the paving look its best.

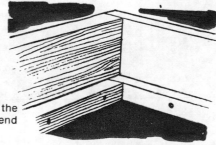

Fig. 11-11. The 1×2s go along the bottom edges of the side and end pieces. (Courtesy Homelite.)

Fig. 11-12. Cutting wood discs. (Courtesy Homelite.)

Flagpoles can be a way to demonstrate pride, but they can also be very troublesome—as when the halyards get hung up at the top pulley and when the pole needs painting. The folding flagpole (Fig. 11-14) makes life much simpler. And it can be built in a short time with your chain saw.

Picnic tables become more and more expensive with each passing year. But with a chain saw, it's quite easy to use trees from your own land or trees someone else wants to cut down.

Fig. 11-13. A patio surface of wood discs. (Courtesy Homelite.)

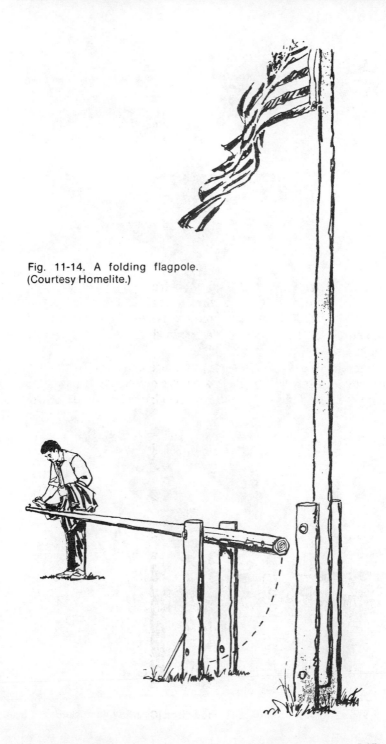

Fig. 11-14. A folding flagpole. (Courtesy Homelite.)

Fig. 11-15. A chain saw can help you create a picnic table at minimal cost. (Courtesy Homelite.)

Fig. 11-16. Detail of picnic table legs. (Courtesy Homelite.)

The wood for a picnic table and benches can be made of lumber cut freehand with your chain saw or Mini-Mill (Fig. 11-15 and 11-16).

These ideas should get you started. Ideas of your own will occur as you go along.

Index